Alexan<
The Ag<

Francis Johnston

Alexandrina
The Agony and the Glory

Translation assistance
by Anne Croshaw

TAN Books and Publishers, Inc.
Rockford, Illinois

Nihil Obstat:
    Richard Sherry, DD
    Censor Deputatus

Imprimatur:
✠ Dermot
    Archbishop of Dublin
    January 1979

The *nihil obstat* and *imprimatur* are a declaration that a text is considered free of doctrinal or moral error. They do not necessarily imply agreement with opinions expressed by the author.

First published in 1979 by
Veritas Publications
7-8 Lower Abbey Street
Dublin 1, Ireland

ISBN: 0-89555-179-9

Printed and bound in the United States of America

TAN Books and Publishers, Inc.
P.O. Box 424
Rockford, Illinois 61105

1982

TO
UMBERTO PASQUALE SDB
IN GRATITUDE

ACKNOWLEDGEMENTS

This first English language book on the Servant of God Alexandrina da Costa owes much to the excellent Italian biography *Alexandrina*, Libreria Dottrina Cristiana, Turin, 1960, by Fr Umberto Pasquale SDB, the noted Salesian writer, to whom grateful acknowledgement is made for permission to use selected excerpts including passages from Alexandrina's autobiography. Fr Pasquale was uniquely qualified to undertake this work, having been Alexandrina's spiritual director for a number of years, besides being a close friend of Sister Lucia, the last survivor of the three children to whom the Mother of God appeared at Fatima in 1917. The translations were effected by Mrs Anne Croshaw for whose invaluable assistance I am deeply grateful.

F.J.

Contents

DECLARATION

In accordance with the decree of Pope Urban VIII, we declare that in speaking of events, prodigies and revelations in this work, we wish to accord them no other authority or belief than that which is usually given to narratives resting on merely human evidence and we in no way presume to pronounce on their authenticity or supernatural character, or to anticipate the judgement of the Holy See.

Prologue

In the main square of the small Portuguese village of Balasar, some forty miles north of Oporto, stands a small chapel dedicated to the Holy Cross. Erected in 1832, it commemorates the mysterious appearance that year of a cross in the village. The parish priest of Balasar at that time, Don A. G. de Azevedo, recorded the event in a report addressed to Rev. Dr A. P. de Azevedo Loureiro of the Archdiocese of Braga.

> I write to advise you of an inexplicable occurrence in this parish of St Eulalia of Balasar. Last Corpus Christi, while the people coming to the morning Mass were passing the road which crosses the little hill of Calvary, they noticed a cross laid out on the ground. The earth which formed this cross was of a lighter colour than the surrounding soil. Dew had fallen all around, except on the cross. I myself went to brush away the dust and loose earth that formed the cross, but the design reappeared in the same place. I then ordered a considerable quantity of water to be poured over it and on the surrounding ground. But after this had drained away, the cross reappeared once more and has remained there since. The staff of the cross measures 15 hands and the transverse measures 8 hands . . .

Many people flocked to see this strange phenomenon and venerated it with flowers and offerings of money. The latter went towards the building of the small chapel mentioned above. The cross remains to this day and still defies attempts to obliterate it.

In the writings of the Servant of God, Alexandrina da Costa, there are three references to this cross, the last of which was dated 14 January 1955. While in ecstasy, she reputedly heard Our Lord say,

> A century ago, I showed the cross to this beloved village, the cross which comes to await the victim. O Balasar, if you do not respond! . . . Cross of earth for the victim who was taken from nothing. . . . Victim who is welcomed by God and who has always existed in his eternal designs. Victim of the world, but much favoured by heavenly blessings, who has given all to Heaven and for the love of souls accepts all. Trust, believe, my daughter, I am here! All your life is written and sealed with a key of gold . . .

The interior of the Chapel of the Holy Cross which commemorates the mysterious appearance of the design of a large cross in the soil at Balasar. Alexandrina's writings contain three references to this cross, which remains visible to this day.

1

Early years

Lying in a trough of gently sloping, pine-wooded hills some seven miles east of the ocean resort of Povoa de Varzim, the village of Balasar consists of irregular clusters of small, rough stone houses, many of them gaudily painted, embracing a population in excess of 1,000 inhabitants. The surrounding countryside is dotted with little white cottages and crowded with vineyards and smallholdings yielding corn, vegetables, olives and figs. Bronze-faced peasants till the stony soil and herd flocks of sheep, goats and amber-coated oxen with lyre-shaped horns and carved yokes along dusty roads, past crumbling tower walls and innumerable trellises and tunnels of vines.

The hamlets and villages of this pleasant region are clustered around their ancient stone churches and Balasar is no exception. Rising on the lower slope of a small stream known as the Este, the parish church of St Eulalia stands like a granite sentinel over the straggling stone houses of Balasar and it was here on 2 April 1904 that Alexandrina Maria da Costa was baptised, having been born four days earlier on the Wednesday of Holy Week, the second child of devout, hard-working peasants.

Shortly after her birth her mother was widowed and Alexandrina grew up with her elder sister Deolinda in an atmosphere of rustic simplicity and piety. As a small child, she must have been fascinated by the colourful religious processions which wound through the village on great feast days and the frequent fairs and dances held in the cobbled market-square to the shrill sound of fifes and accordians and a kaleidoscope of floral blouses, twirling skirts and flashing earrings.

Her earliest memory was when she was three years old. As she lay in bed with her mother for the afternoon siesta, she noticed a small jar of pomade on a nearby table. Carefully, so as not to waken her mother, she reached out for the jar with inquisitive hands. At that moment, the sleeping woman roused herself and called Alexandrina. Taken by surprise, the child let the jar fall to the floor where it shattered to pieces. Losing her balance, Alexandrina toppled over, injuring the corner of her mouth. She carried the scar for the rest of her life.

Naturally, she shrieked with pain and would not be comforted. Her mother, Maria Anna, anxiously wiped the blood from her mouth and quickly ran her to the nearby chemist shop for a prescription, where a kindly assistant tried to calm the child with a bag of sweets. Alexandrina responded with yells, kicks and scratches. "That was my first misdemeanour", she wrote in her autobiography which she began dictating to Deolinda in 1940 at the request of her spiritual director, Fr Pinho, SJ.

As she grew older, she would wander, fascinated, through the ancient village church contemplating the beautiful statues of the saints, particularly that of Our Lady of the Rosary and St Joseph. Their rich costumes enchanted her and she dreamed of dressing in the same way. "Perhaps this was a manifestation of my vanity", she wryly commented later.

One day when she was about six, she was overjoyed to receive a little pair of wooden shoes from her mother. In a transport of happiness she danced into her room dressed in her best clothes, and putting on the shoes, strutted around the house like a peacock. Having tired of this, she knelt down on the pavement outside and proudly placed the shoes in front of her as women did in the churches of Portuguese villages in those days.

One of her most formative experiences was vividly described by her years later.

When our uncle died, **Deolinda** and I stayed with his family until the seventh day after his death, to assist at the Requiem Mass. One morning, I was asked to go and get some rice from a bag which was in the room where his body lay. When I reached the door, I was unable to muster up the courage to enter. I was frightened. So my grandmother had to get the rice. That same evening I was ordered to go and close the window of that room. As I reached the door, I felt my knees tremble again and was unable to enter. Then I said to myself, "I must fight it. I must overcome the fear." I opened the door and slowly walked into the room where my uncle lay. Since that day, I have been able to master my sense of fear.

Her inborn liveliness and sense of humour led her to become a gay tomboy, full of wit and laughter, though without compromising a budding spirituality which few suspected, judging from her spontaneous joviality. Witty phrases and lively jokes flowed from her laughing lips. Deolinda, who was more composed by nature, was nearly always the victim. One morning, Alexandrina pushed over the lid of a large box of bed-linens and screamed as if she had crushed her hand. Deolinda rushed to her aid in panic, to be met by a chortle of laughter. In church, she would furtively tie together the fringes of women's shawls as they listened attentively to the sermon. Outside after Mass, she would hide behind a low wall and throw stones at the people emerging from the church.

Gradually, her developing spirituality began to master her propensity for mischief. By the time of her first Communion at the age of seven, she had already acquired a deep love of the Blessed Sacrament, visiting the village church with unusual frequency and making spiritual Communions whenever she was unable to attend Mass. On Sundays, she loved to sing in the choir and participate in the parish catechism group. When an aunt suffering from cancer begged Alexandrina to pray for her, the child responded with such fervour and perseverance that the habit of prayer became entrenched in her young soul. She wrote later:

I always had a great respect for priests. Sometimes, when I used to sit on a doorstep at Povoa de Varzim and see priests walking by in the street . . . I used to stand with respect as they passed. They would take off their hats to me and say the customary "God bless you." I often noticed that people looked at me as I did this. Sometimes I sat there on purpose so that I could get up at the appropriate moment to show my veneration for priests.

When Alexandrina was nine, she went with Deolinda and a cousin to hear a sermon in a nearby village given by a famous preacher, Fr Emmanuel of the Holy Wounds. She made her first general confession to him and the three girls remained there all day to listen to the afternoon sermon. Having taken their seats at the side of the Sacred Heart altar, Alexandrina placed her wooden shoes between the columns of the balustrade and listened to the priest with rapt attention. She recalled:

At a certain point the priest invited us to descend in spirit to the place of eternal suffering – Hell. I was incapable of understanding the exact meaning of this invitation, and convinced that the priest was a saint, I thought he would actually take us down to Hell. I rebelled and said to myself, "I don't want to go to Hell. If the others want to go there, I'm staying behind." I immediately took hold of my wooden shoes and made ready to escape. When I noticed that nobody was moving, I quietened down a little, but I kept a tight hold of my wooden shoes.

Due to the restrictions of rural life in those days, Alexandrina had only eighteen months schooling before being sent to work on a farm at the age of nine. Though a strong, capable child, the heavy manual labour, shot through with incessant bad language, taxed her severely. When she was twelve, her employer tried to assault her. She fought back vigorously and somehow managed to drive him off with an unexplained force in her rosary-clenched fist.

After this serious incident she was promptly brought home. This gave her the opportunity to become a daily communicant and to renew her love and devotion to the Blessed Sacrament. But later that year she fell dangerously

ill with typhoid. Her condition became critical; for several
days she hovered on the brink of death. When her weeping
mother gave her a crucifix to kiss, Alexandrina shook her
head and murmured, "This is not what I want, but Jesus in
the Eucharist."

She finally recovered and was sent to a sanatorium at
Povoa de Varzim on the bracing Atlantic coast. But her
health remained precarious, and when she returned to
Balasar she was still a virtual invalid. This led her to take up
sewing for a living and she settled down in the village learn-
ing to be a seamstress with her sister.

One day when she was fourteen, she heard that the
father of one of her friends had been found dying. She
hurried to where he was living alone and found him lying
in a heap of rags. Filled with compassion, she ran back to
her mother and borrowing soap, towels and bed-linen,
restored a semblance of human dignity to the poor man.
He lived on for another twelve days and Alexandrina
remained with him until the end to comfort him and his
grief-stricken daughter.

Shortly after, her role of good Samaritan was repeated.
She recalled in her autobiography:

A neighbour warned us that an old lady was dying. My
sister took her prayer-book and some holy water and left
the house. I followed her with two of my sister's sewing
pupils.

At the door was a niece of the sick woman who did
not have the courage to assist her. Deolinda entered and
began to read the prayers for the dying over the woman.
I stood at her side and I noticed that the fringe of her
shawl was trembling like a leaf. When she had finished
reading the prayers the daughter entered, but the old
lady breathed her last without recognising her.

Deolinda then took her leave, saying "I have done all
I can; I have no more courage to stay on." On seeing the
dead woman's daughter in anguish, I hadn't the heart to
leave her alone. I decided to remain and help her to wash
and lay out the body, which was covered with sores. The
smell was dreadful . . . and I had the feeling that I was

going to faint. I said nothing, however, but a woman
who had joined us noticed my distress and went to get a
twig of geranium so that I could smell it. I thanked her
sincerely, but did not interrupt my work. I finally left,
after the body of the dead woman had been arranged
with dignity.

One day, while Alexandrina was praying alone in her
house, she heard the door of the courtyard open and
moments later, a man's voice demanded, "Open that door!"
Recognising it as that of her former employer, and realising
she had no means to lock herself in, she clutched her rosary
in apprehension and waited for the man to enter. There was
a succession of violent rattles as he hammered at the
unlocked door. But it refused to open. After vainly trying
to force his way inside, the exasperated man finally went
off, leaving the shaken girl convinced that Our Lord and his
mother had barred the way to protect her chastity.

2

Victim soul

Alexandrina might have remained in the undramatic capacity of a seamstress, buried away in the wild and beautiful Portuguese countryside, had not a fateful event occurred in March 1918 which utterly transformed her life.

While she was working one day in an upstairs room in her home with Deolinda and another girl, there was a sudden knock at the front door. Alexandrina peered through the window, and to her dismay saw three men standing outside, one of whom was her former employer again. A glance at their impassioned faces told her the worst. She locked the door of the room at once. The men broke into the house and began forcing open a trapdoor on the floor of the upstairs room.

The girls quickly moved a heavy sewing-machine over the trap door. Not to be thwarted so easily, the men pounded the door with clubs. The dry wood splintered, the sewing-machine toppled over. One by one, the men levered themselves into the room. Deolinda and her friend were seized and Alexandrina was cornered by a third man.

"Jesus help me!" she screamed, lashing out at him with her rosary. Like St Maria Goretti, she was ready to die rather than consent to the man's lust. Frantically, she looked round for a way of escape. Behind her was a window, thirteen feet above the hard ground. It was her one chance. Desperately she jumped.

The pain was shattering. Gritting her teeth and wiping the blood from her face, she seized a stout piece of wood and staggered back into the house to defend her companions. Several well-aimed blows were enough. The startled men took to their heels, bruised and shaken by her

The thirteen-foot high window from which Alexandrina jumped in order to escape from a man who had come to molest her. This event occurred when Alexandrina was fourteen years old; it resulted in a spinal injury which eventually led to total paralysis at the age of twenty.

The da Costa home, where the bedridden Alexandrina was confined to a tiny upstairs room.

courageous counter-attack. Fortunately, the other two girls were unmolested.

But Alexandrina's spine had been irreparably injured. Long months of increasing pain, incapacity and depression followed, though she never yielded to despair. In 1923 a specialist from Oporto, Dr Joao de Almeida, confirmed the family's worst fears. Total paralysis set in and on 14 April 1924 she became bedridden for life.

The awful predicament clutched at her heart and severely tested her faith and courage. Confined to a tiny upstairs room in an obscure house hidden from the outside world by a high stone wall was tantamount to being buried alive. Fortunately she had already practised the virtue of detachment; her only desire being for flowers and for the church. Deolinda settled down to become her nurse and secretary while their mother worked to earn money for food. "I had moments of discouragement," Alexandrina says of this period, "but never one of despair." When there were singing lessons in the church, the two sisters became sad, one because she had to leave her charge and the other because she could not go. But the crippled heroine conformed very quickly to the will of God and regarded her bed as "my beloved cross".

At first, she tried to distract herself by inviting friends in for a game of cards. But the novelty soon wore off and she resolved to try to storm heaven for a cure. She promised to give away everything she had, to dress herself in mourning for the rest of her life, to cut off her hair, if only she was cured. Her anguished family and cousins joined in the assault on heaven, but the paralysis stayed.

Worse still, her condition began to deteriorate until the slightest movement caused her agonising pain. Once again she hovered on the brink of death, and the last sacraments were administered several times. The medicine she took had no effect, except to soothe and calm her. Looking back at this distressing period she wrote later that "I would have done better to have stayed united to Jesus because he alone is the true life and the true joy."

Every evening the Costa family gathered round her bed and lighting two candles before the statue of Our Lady, recited the rosary on their knees, followed by night prayers. During the day, whenever there were no companions to distract her, Alexandrina would meditate, pray and weep, imploring Our Lady to heal her. Sadly, she would sing the *Tantum Ergo* as in church, and not having the blessing of Benediction, she would ask Jesus for it from heaven, "and from all the tabernacles in the world". The parish priest lent her a statue of the Immaculate Heart of Mary for the month of May, and afterwards Alexandrina scraped together every penny she could to buy a similar statue of her own. In time, this statue was almost kissed smooth.

Her growing love of prayer led her to abandon her innocent distractions. She began to long for a life of union with Jesus. This union, she perceived, could only be realised by bearing her illness and incapacity for love of him. The idea of suffering being her vocation suddenly dawned on her. Without knowing how, she offered herself to God as a victim soul for the conversion of sinners.

In 1928, a local pilgrimage to Fatima was organised and Alexandrina implored Our Lady to let her accompany them. The fast-growing shrine was already a magnet for hundreds of thousands on the thirteenth of each month from May to October, and the numerous miracles occurring there gave the sick woman a surge of hope. But the doctor and parish priest were adamantly opposed to the idea. How could she be conveyed some 200 miles, they argued, if to touch or turn her caused her unspeakable suffering?

In the face of their inflexible stand, Alexandrina brokenly closed her eyes in prayer and offered to God the crushing sacrifice of her abandonment and isolation. Gazing fixedly at the statue of Our Lady, she prayed her heart out for a cure at home. She promised that on being healed, she would become a missionary and she told her friends that if they heard singing in the streets, it would be her thanking God and Our Lady for a miracle.

Week after week she prayed imploringly. Month after month she pleaded and wept for a cure. But the paralysis remained. Gradually, little by little, the desire for recovery died in her and she began to think only of loving God. As she prayed, her thoughts strayed longingly across to the Blessed Sacrament in the nearby church, and suddenly she realised that Our Lord in the tabernacle was also a prisoner.

This touching link with Christ led her to visit him in spirit, to remain constantly before him in union with Our Lady, keeping watch with unceasing love, prayer and self-immolation, to console his Sacred Heart and obtain the conversion of sinners. *To Jesus through Mary* became her constant watchword. For long hours she meditated on the spiritual crisis in the world until she was fully conscious of the enormity of modern sin and the crying need for its expiation in union with the suffering Christ.

Pope Pius XI had underscored this need that very year in his encyclical *Miserentissimus Redemptor*. His Holiness wrote:

Although the copious Redemption operated by Our Lord has superabundantly forgiven all sins, yet through that admirable disposition of Divine Wisdom, there must be completed in us what is missing in Christ's suffering on behalf of his Body, that is, his Church *(Col 1:24)*. We can and we must add to the homage and satisfaction (expiratory suffering) that Christ renders to God, our own homage and satisfactions on behalf of sinners. . . . While men's malice incessantly increases, the breath of the Holy Spirit wonderfully multiplies the number of the faithful who generously try to repair so many outrages made to the Divine Heart, and they even do not hesitate in offering themselves to Christ as victims. . . .

Alexandrina realised that while this vocation applied to everyone in an elementary degree, the intense reparation of a victim soul was a very special vocation, reserved by God for the favoured few. The deeper she pondered, the more she became convinced that this was her exalted vocation. With a surge of tearful love, she implored Our Lord to accept her as his victim, to allow her to stand as a surety for sinners before the bar of divine justice, to cause her to suffer to the limit of her endurance if thereby sinners could excape hell.

Seemingly in response to this remarkably courageous request, her pain steadily intensified until it became almost unendurable. Night after feverish night she would lie awake gasping and struggling to pray, her head soaking the pillow, her fingers clenching her rosary with tight desperation as if squeezing relief from the clamped beads. "O Jesus," she would pant, repeating the prayer taught by Our Lady at Fatima, "this is for love of thee, for the conversion of sinners, and in reparation for the offences against the Immaculate Heart of Mary."

Despite the fierceness of her pangs, she persevered with her prayerful oblation, day after interminable day, month after prolonged month. Her ardent devotion to Our Lady, which she had cultivated since childhood, became a springboard from which she was able to leap more securely into the arms of Christ. She asked for a little altar to be fixed to the wall by her bed where it was graced with the statue of Our Lady of Fatima and decorated with flowers and candles. During each month of May, she tried to make herself the most beautiful flower of May by offering little "spiritual flowers" to the mother of God. She would offer the whole day with its sufferings, and her intentions would range from the needs of the parish to those of the entire world. At the end of the month she placed these petitions at the feet of the statue, together with an affectionate letter to Our Lady. One such letter read:

Little Mother, I come humbly to your feet to lay down the little spiritual flowers which I have collected during this month. Behold the state in which I offer them to you! They are so faded and leafless. But you, O Heavenly Mother, could transform them. Speak to your Divine Son of my distress and affliction. . . . Repeat to him on my behalf all my supplications, and grant that my poor flowers may be acceptable, so as to benefit those for whom they were offered. In particular, I beg you to make a beautiful garland of them to offer to the Holy Father on his birthday.

Mother dear, on the last day of your blessed month, since I have nothing to offer you, I give you my whole body. I ask you to take charge of it and take it on your arm as you would take that of a beloved daughter. Bless me, dear Mother. Ask Jesus in the Blessed Sacrament to bless me. Ask the Holy Trinity to bless me. Goodbye dear Mother, and forgive me everything.

Every day in May she recited the following act of consecration to the Blessed Virgin:

Mother of Jesus and my Mother, listen to my prayer. I consecrate my body and all my heart to you. Purify me, most holy Mother; fill me with your holy love. Place me near the tabernacle of Jesus in order that I can serve as a lamp as long as the world lasts. Bless me, sanctify me, O dear Mother of Heaven!

Many times during the long and lonely days she would turn her thoughts to the tabernacle in the village church, and repeat:

My good Jesus, you are a prisoner and I am a prisoner. We are both prisoners. You are a prisoner for my welfare and happiness and I am a prisoner of your hands. You are King and Lord of all and I am a worm of the earth. I have abandoned you, thinking only of this world which is the destruction of souls. But now, repenting with all my heart, I desire only that which you desire, and to suffer with resignation. O my Jesus, I adore thee everywhere thou dwellest in the Blessed Sacrament. Where thou art despised, I stand by thee. I love thee for those who do not love. I make amends for those who offend thee. Come into my heart.

Her severe pain continued with only occasional periods of relative relief. Frequently she was seen quivering and moaning with agony. Finally in 1931, the throbbing red haze dissolved and for the first time she entered into a state of ecstasy. Reputedly, she heard the voice of Christ overflowing with love and tenderness, inviting her to "Love, suffer and make reparation." Alexandrina bravely and generously consented. She begged Our Lord to give her renewed strength and patience to endure on behalf of sinners whatever further sufferings he might have in store for her.

She did not have long to wait for an answer. The priest who brought her daily Communion was replaced by a Fr Mateus, a strict, legalistic priest who maintained on principle that she should only be permitted to receive Communion on the first Friday of each month. The anguish of being deprived of her beloved Eucharist was almost more than she could bear. The daily visit of Our Lord had been the one thing that had kept her spirit going. Tearfully, she begged the priest to come more frequently, meanwhile offering the sacrifice for those who neglected the Bread of Life. Finally, Fr Mateus relented slightly and agreed to come every fifteen days.

3

Ascent to Calvary

As the long painful months stretched into years, Alexandrina began to yearn for the holy sacrifice of the Mass to be celebrated in her humble room. It seemed to her to be a grace beyond attainment and she kept the desire to herself. But in the autumn of 1933, on hearing that a holy Jesuit priest, Fr Mariano Pinho, would be preaching in the district, she told Deolinda of her ardent wish. The latter promised to do what she could.

Shortly after, the parish priest wrote and asked Alexandrina if it would please her to assist at Holy Mass. She replied at once, "It would be such a joy for me that I do not know how to express myself, but it would be a great hardship for any priest to come fasting on such a cold morning. . . ." And so it was on 20 November 1933 that Fr Pinho SJ celebrated the first Mass in her little room, now the goal for pilgrims from all over the world. Though Mass was to be said there many times later, Alexandrina never quite recaptured the trembling joy of the first occasion. "With that first Mass," she said afterwards, "Our Lord began to increase his tenderness towards me, and at the same time the weight of my cross. Blessed be the grace which, in his goodness, is never lacking to me."

Conscious of the workings of divine love in her soul, and at the same time confused by such undeserved generosity of God, Alexandrina asked Our Lord why he was lowering himself to a sinner like her. In the depths of her soul she seemed to hear him answer, "I do not do this only to holy souls; I communicate myself even to the souls of sinners like you, to give them faith in me, for even sinners

27

can love me and become saints. If I did not do this, they would have reason to despair."

When she later disclosed these words to her spiritual director, she added with childish simplicity:

> I paid much attention to his words and wondered how I would understand and explain them . . . because my head does not serve me very well. But Our Lord told me that the Holy Spirit would come upon me and his light would inspire me to understand and explain everything.

Shortly after the first Mass had been celebrated in her room, she reputedly received a vision of Christ. Here is her account of that memorable occasion:

> One night Jesus appeared to me in natural dimensions, as if he had just been taken down from the cross. I could see deep, open wounds in his hands, his feet and his side. The Blood streamed from these wounds, and from the breast it came with such force that, after having drenched the garment around his waist, it flooded onto the floor. Jesus drew near to the edge of my bed. With great love I was able to kiss the wounds in his hands and I longed to kiss those in his feet. But due to my paralysis, I was unable to do so. Though I said nothing of this desire to Jesus, he knew what was in my mind and with his hands he held up one foot and then the other and offered them to me to kiss. . . . Enraptured, I contemplated the wound in his side and the Blood that was gushing from it until, filled with compassion, I threw myself into his arms and cried out, "O my Jesus, how much you have suffered for me!" I remained in his arms for some moments and he finally disappeared.

This sublime vision left an indelible impression on Alexandrina: even many years later, its memory was so vivid that it still seemed to be visible to her.

A word is necessary here concerning the reputed visions of Alexandrina. In 1945, she replied to a question on them by Fr Pasquale SDB (who succeeded Fr Pinho SJ as her spiritual director) as follows: "I see in three different ways. Sometimes like one who sees an image, an earthly person.

At other times I see with the interior eyes of the soul. . . ."
Indicating the third and highest form of perception she said,
"At other times, I see as if I had other eyes, and not even
those of the spirit." So saying, she touched her heart and
added, "It is not with this." And touching her forehead,
"Nor even with this." She went on, "It is not to see with
the eyes and not even with the mind, but it is like a clear
light which sees and understands everything." Commented
Fr Pasquale, "She sees as if she has other eyes: it is 'intellectual vision', through which her mind receives in itself the
shining splendour of Eternal Truth and Eternal Beauty."

Alexandrina went on:

> I do not understand the things which Jesus says to me as
> we understand the expressions of people. It is as if I had
> in front of me a picture with the things which he wants
> to tell me, as if everything were written in front of me,
> but that I read everything at the same time.

Fr Pasquale was astonished at such a precise explanation
of mystical intuition, bearing in mind that she was an almost
illiterate peasant woman, completely devoid of specialised
theological and mystical readings. "Divine symphony," he
marvelled, "which, in the gentle modulation of the illuminat-
ing Voice, makes her feel in the eternal moment, the
inexhaustible riches of that which then unfolds with the
rhythm which time pronounces clearly, slowly and labor-
iously."

Alexandrina could also reproduce every word spoken to
her in a vision with unerring accuracy, *without altering a
syllable,* months afterwards. During many of her later
ecstasies, while she spoke, or Jesus reputedly spoke through
her mouth, Fr Pasquale would write everything down.
When the ecstasy was over, he would read back to her what
he had written, deliberately modifying some verb, name or
adjective to put her to the test. Alexandrina would unfail-
ingly correct him saying sweetly, "I did not say that", or
"Jesus did not say that." She would then add, "Write
this . . ." repeating exactly what the priest had written.

Shortly after the first Mass in the sickroom, Deolinda undertook a course of exercises for the Children of Mary during which she chose Fr Pinho to be her spiritual director. She reminded him of her bedridden sister and he promised to pray for her, asking for her prayers in return. A few days later he visited Alexandrina and at her request, agreed to become spiritual director to both sisters.

For a year the sick woman remained undecided about whether to tell him of her offering to the Blessed Sacrament, of the burning heat which she was beginning to feel, of the mysterious strength which elevated her, and of the words which she believed she had heard from Jesus. Her reserve with Fr Pinho distressed her, but when she finally opened her soul to him, she was tormented by the conviction that the priest would abandon her. A few days later, however, she had an ecstasy in which she seemed to hear Jesus telling her, "Obey your spiritual father in everything. You have not chosen him; it was I who sent him to you."

Meanwhile Alexandrina's acute sufferings persisted, as if her body had become a veritable instrument of torture. Only occasionally did she reveal the fierceness of her pain to Deolinda or Fr Pinho. Now that writing had become virtually impossible for her, she dictated to her sister most of her letters to the Jesuit. The passages quoted here give a graphic idea of the ordeal through which she was passing.

Just a few words because my strength does not permit more. I passed the night badly. I could not find a position. So the days pass, one better and another worse, with this cross which Our Lord gives me. (6.11.1933.)

In the night from Saturday to Sunday, I do not know what passed through my head. I was sleeping and I awoke: I seemed to die. This strange phenomenon lasted but a short while, but it repeated itself often. I think it was caused by my backbone. I hope Our Lord listens to me, but his Holy Will be done. . . . Very often I ask, "O my Jesus, what do you wish me to do?" And every time I listen I hear only this answer, "Suffer, love and make reparation." (28.3.1933.)

Blessed be the Lord who has called me into this world in order to suffer and bear so many tribulations! To all this, I unite many sins which grieve me more than anything else. I ask every day for suffering and I feel great spiritual consolation when I suffer more, because I have more to offer to my Jesus. However, there are things which cost so much, but God's Will, not mine be done. (30.12.1933.)

My suffering has increased considerably and I can now take only liquids due to a swelling in my mouth. Maybe as it has come, so it will go away. With the weakness in which I find myself, it will be impossible for me to live very long. . . . The lack of food causes me further suffering while liquids often cause me to vomit. I ask God every day not to abandon me for a moment, knowing well that without him I could not bear anything. (8.3.1934.)

I would like to thank you for your birthday greetings by my own hand and I do it by writing a few lines. They will certainly be my last. I ask pardon, I cannot continue. *(She gives the pen to her sister.)* My suffering has increased still more. It is because of this that these will be the last lines which I write to you. It is impossible to hold the pen for even a few moments, the pain is so great. I had a beautiful Easter present from Jesus: besides physical suffering, he has given me spiritual suffering." (7.4.1934.)

Two months later in another letter, she spoke of the displacement of some of her ribs and added:

I cannot lean on them without great pain, nor bear the garments over them. . . . Does everything contrary come from God, or could they come from the devil, since there have been incidents in my life which appear to be his work. (22.6.1934.)

This reference to the devil was the first indication of the diabolic assaults from which she was beginning to suffer.

On the feast of Our Lady of Mount Carmel 1934 she wrote,

> I have the impression that the ribs of the breast have united to those of the back, causing me such great agony that I do not know how to bear it. When the pain is unendurable, I find half my body lying on the bed and the other half on Deolinda's lap. This obliges my sister to pass whole nights in my company. It even costs me a lot to speak.

In a nearby village, a religious festival was profaned by amusements and Alexandrina wrote,

> I have repeated to Jesus: send me as much suffering as you wish, provided that I can make reparation for the offences which you receive. (15.8.1934.)

A few days later she wrote,

> I do not know if it is through the prayers you offer for me that I feel stronger each day in my sufferings. I seem to have courage to suffer more and I hope that the Lord will, little by little, increase the pain until I die, inflamed by his Divine Love and nailed to the cross with him.

It should be emphasised here that Alexandrina revealed the intensity of her sufferings to no one but Fr Pinho and Deolinda, who became her confidante. Her mother was ignorant of much of what happened in that little room. With the same zeal, Alexandrina concealed the charisms given to her soul by a fine sense of humility and by the fear that she would be disbelieved. From the day she offered herself as a victim soul, she repeated the following prayer continually: "O Jesus, place on my lips a deceiving smile in which I can hide all the martyrdom of my soul. It is enough that only you know of my endurance."

As a result, those who visited her saw only a courageous smile which effectively masked her dreadful pain. A priest who knew her at this time testified:

> Among the many reasons which arouse the admiration of visitors is her enchanting simplicity, her angelic purity

and above all, the clearness of mind and the perspicacity of her spirit. Whoever speaks to her does not have the impression of speaking to a sick person who suffers a great deal, physically and morally, because Alexandrina knows how to conceal her suffering beneath a smile. . . . Every visitor leaves that little room perfectly deceived.

About this time, the Costa family passed through a period of grinding poverty due to the generosity of their mother, who made herself trustee to a number of needy persons in the village. Alexandrina admitted later:

I suffered bitterly, seeing that everything we possessed was insufficient to pay off the debts of those for whom my mother had made herself trustee. I told my family that I preferred to lose our last cent so that all our debts could be paid. I often lacked the nourishing food I needed, but I suffered in silence. Since I never asked for anything that was not in the house, my family were persuaded that everything I ate was to my taste. If they gave me something extra, I passed it at once to Deolinda who was very delicate at the time. I reasoned, "If my recovery is not possible, I can at least make Deolinda better." The family suffered real privations, such as having to cook the soup without condiments, but we told nobody of our trials. At night I would weep and find consolation only with Jesus and his holy Mother. Blessed tears that united me more closely to God every hour. . . . The sole thought that gave me resignation and joy was that Jesus wanted us to live in poverty in order to be more like him. . . .

In her prayers after Communion, she remembered the promise of Jesus, "Ask and you shall receive." So she implored Our Lord, "Jesus, assist us or we perish. Carry far this petition to someone who can help us." Six years of sadness and tears passed. In the family there was scarcely a moment of serenity. Finally her prayers were answered. A good lady (Signora Fernando Santos of Lisbon) from the other side of the country came to relieve their troubles and gave them a sufficient sum of money to prevent them from selling their house. "I wept with confusion and joy", said

Alexandrina. "I did not know how to thank Our Lord for
so much grace."

On 6 September 1934 Alexandrina experienced a
wonderful ecstasy, in which the compassionate voice of
Christ seemed to invite her to draw closer to his Sacred
Heart and share in the intense fire of his redeeming pain:

> Give me your hands, because I want to nail them with
> mine. Give me your feet, because I want to nail them to
> my feet. Give me your head, because I want to crown it
> with thorns as they did to me. Give me your heart,
> because I want to pierce it with a lance as they pierced
> mine. Consecrate your body to me; offer yourself wholly
> to me. . . . Help me in the redemption of mankind.

Alexandrina bravely and generously consented, though
she remained bewildered by the meaning of these mysterious
words. But as the weeks went by, the fierceness of her
suffering seemed to intensify until her life became a furnace
of excruciating agony. Amid the white-hot bolts of pain,
Our Lord made himself the teacher and "artist" of her soul,
as he had done to St Margaret Mary in the 17th century.
She reputedly had further visions in which Jesus presented
himself to her under different aspects, sometimes with his
Sacred Heart surrounded by rays of love. At other times he
showed her his mother, streaming with light. More and
more, she felt the need to be alone; her soul passed through
a period of such spiritual consolation that she was able to
bear her atrocious pain with greater fortitude and resignation.

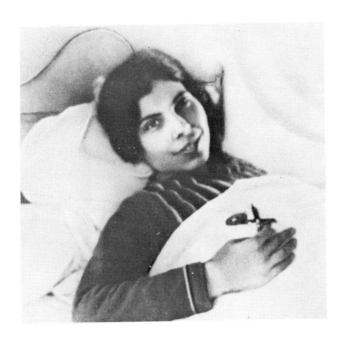

Alexandrina in 1935 at the age of thirty-one, shortly after the devil began his terrible temptations and savage attacks, which were to last for about ten years.

4

Years of torment

Alexandrina's life of suffering in expiation for sin was now to be challenged by the powers of darkness. From 1934 onwards, she began to be assailed by hideous visions and howling, blasphemous taunts that God had abandoned her, that suicide was the imperative alternative to a life of agonising futility. Realising that the spirit of Satan is primarily one of rebellion, she placed her will entirely in the hands of her spiritual director and never once took it back, even when it cost her a great deal.

Whenever Fr Pinho was unable to visit her, he asked Alexandrina to inform him of everything that happened to her. On 14 September 1934 she wrote to him as follows:

> Do you want to know what that "black face from Hell" recently beat into my head? Here it is: "Whatever I write to you will be the cause of my condemnation . . . and that if I do not obey him . . . the worst will happen." It makes me weep.

Seeing her so afflicted, Our Lord reportedly appeared to her a month later and said, "Whom do you wish to obey, me and your director – or the devil?" His words reassured Alexandrina, but the devil returned to the attack. He raved:

> Excommunication, a thousand excommunications if you continue to write to your spiritual director! Already you are burning in Hell. Be converted, unhappy one! Be converted, miserable wretch! It is the affection I have for you that makes me speak in this way. I come now from your Christ who told me to take you, because he can no longer save you. He was distressed . . . by your writings.

The devil added that it was useless for her to pray, that there was no salvation for her, that nobody would be able to help her, that she would be condemned.

Alexandrina recalled:

> One moonlit night after prayers I felt a need to sleep, when suddenly into my room came a great darkness. . . . I perceived a black shadow and saw it jump towards me, and it said to me, "I come on behalf of your Christ to carry you to Hell, bed and all." I kissed the crucifix and the voice continued, "You kiss that wicked thing!" He then ordered me to do things that I cannot speak of. . . . It was only when I took holy water that I was left in peace.

She continued:

> Every now and then I see a rapid light. Twice I have seen two very big eyes, wide open, staring at me, but they disappeared quickly. On Sunday, I heard a very sweet voice saying, "My daughter, I come to tell you not to write anything of what you see: your sight is deceiving you. Don't you feel how weak you are? You displease me with this; it is your Jesus who speaks to you, not Satan." I was suspicious and began to kiss the crucifix. The voice became enraged and thundered, "If you continue to write I will destroy your body. Do you think I could not do this?"

In a letter to Fr Pinho dated 14 February 1935, Alexandrina wrote, "The demon wanted me to remove the sacred objects which I wore and the crucifix which I held in my hand. He told me that he had secrets to confide to me, but first I must take off those objects which he hates."

For long periods, while she endured fresh sufferings, Our Lord seemed to have abandoned her, for she no longer heard the reassurance of his voice. The devil exploited this opportunity to the utmost by sowing in her soul the seeds of immense doubt as to the value of her sufferings, by striving to convince her that she would be damned, and by again trying to induce her to commit suicide. "I took holy water, as I have done on similar occasions", she told Fr

Pinho. "I prayed long and earnestly, 'O my Jesus, never, never do I wish to offend you. I resolve in advance not to say or do anything which could offend you.'"

She went on:

> There are days when the devil makes me feel so exhausted and puts so many evil suggestions and doubts into my mind, that were it not for the goodness of God, he would have won me already. . . . He has tempted me so much that on some days I feel that Hell itself is about to engulf me. He urges me to kill myself, and says he will give me the means to do this without any cost. He adds that I am suffering here for no recompense, that Our Lord does not love me at all, that my spiritual director does not believe a word of what I write to him, that what I feel in myself when Our Lord speaks to me is caused by the weather, or by my illness.

Frequently when the seer pressed the crucifix to her lips, the devil would sneer in a threatening voice. Once he raged:

> If it were not for that imposter which you have in your hand, I would put a foot on your neck. I would reduce your body to a pulp. But you will see that he will do this to you himself. You will then wish to come to me, but I will not accept you. Thank that object of superstition. . . . I don't fear it any more, but I hate it!

Alexandrina's courage was repeatedly tested to the full. On 2 February 1935 she spoke of seeing "red beings that I do not know how to describe" and went on, "Alas! If only I had a priest to open my heart to. . . . How can I avoid such distress? I weep, but they are tears of resignation to the holy Will of God."

All this time her physical sufferings continued and her ecstasies grew more numerous and profound. Finally on the feast of the Most Holy Trinity 1936, she passed through her first mystical death — a paroxysm of the most dreadful agony. Fr Mateus was now convinced of the genuineness of her mysticism and as her condition steadily deteriorated, he agreed to bring her Holy Communion every morning.

During this period, she was entrusted by Our Lord with the propagation of the message of Our Lady of Fatima. After she had received Communion one morning Jesus reportedly told her, "Through the love which you have for my blessed Mother, tell your spiritual director that as I asked Margaret Mary [St Margaret Mary Alacoque] for devotion to my divine Heart, so I ask you to urge the consecration of the world to the Immaculate Heart of my Mother." From that day, Alexandrina offered herself as a victim to achieve this expressed wish of Our Lord.

In September 1936, Fr Pinho forwarded to Cardinal Pacelli [later Pope Pius XII] in Rome, Alexandrina's request for the consecration of the world to the Immaculate Heart of Mary. The former was strongly influenced by Our Lord's reported words to the sick woman,

> I reveal to you how the consecration of the world to the Mother of men will occur. It will be effected first by the Holy Father in Rome, and then by priests in all the churches. If the world is converted she will reign, and through her victory will be obtained.

The following year, and again in 1939 the Holy See sent a noted theologian, Fr Paul Durao, to examine Alexandrina and question her closely regarding her reported mysticism and messages. On 5 May 1938, Alexandrina wrote to Fr Pinho, who was preaching the spiritual exercises of St Ignatius to the Portuguese bishops assembled at Fatima: "Jesus has told me, 'I give you the treasures of my Heart overflowing with love; distribute them to the world.' " She added, "I offer everything for the successful outcome of the excercises of the bishops. I help them with the sufferings of my body and soul, which are many."

Significantly, at the end of the exercises, the Portuguese bishops, at the invitation of Fr Pinho, addressed themselves to the Holy Father as follows: "Humbly prostrate at the feet of your Holiness, we earnestly implore you to consecrate the entire world to the Immaculate Heart of Mary as soon as you judge the moment opportune, so that through her mediation, the world can be liberated from the dangers that threaten it on every side."

When news of this petition reached Alexandrina, she was greatly consoled, but shortly after Our Lord told her, "As a sign that it is my Will that the world be consecrated to the Immaculate Heart of my Mother, I will make you suffer my Passion until the Holy Father has decided to implement this consecration." The words mystified Alexandrina, but a few weeks later they were clarified by an awesome event, described in the following chapter.

The war clouds were now gathering all over Europe and in March 1939, Cardinal Pacelli was elected to the papacy as Pope Pius XII. Our Lord told Alexandrina, "This is the pope who will consecrate the world to the Heart of my Mother." In anguished sorrow he went on to deplore the "numberless grave sins" committed all over the world and how Divine Justice had no choice but to "punish mankind". Alexandrina immediately offered herself as a victim for peace "in union with Our Lady". Our Lord accepted her offering and promised that "Portugal will be saved from the war" and that the Holy Father would be "physically spared", but would have to suffer morally a great deal.

Meanwhile the devil continued to assail Alexandrina without respite. Seeing his assaults were making no impression on the sick woman, he redoubled his efforts, resorting even to physical violence, as he had done to the Curé of Ars a century earlier. She describes the harrowing ordeal as follows:

It was in July 1937 that the devil, finding he was making no headway by tormenting my conscience and making vile suggestions, began to hurl me from the bed, sometimes at night and sometimes during the day. In the beginning I concealed these attacks from my family, with the exception of Deolinda. But as the violence of the evil one increased, I felt obliged to tell my mother and the girl we had at home. Those who saw my bruises after the falls were distressed, but they had no idea of the true cause. As the days passed, things went from bad to worse. Deolinda was compelled to sleep on a mattress near my bed, and one night the devil hurled me against the wall so that I fell onto my sister's couch. Deolinda rose and taking hold of me, ordered imperiously, "Up, up to bed!" and put me back to bed. I arose again and gave a shrill whistle. Then realising what I had done, I began to weep. Deolinda quietened me. "Don't upset yourself, it is not you", she said. The following night the same thing happened again and when my sister tried to put me back to bed, I shouted "I don't want to!" and pushed her away from me.

One night, when the devil flung me into different corners of the room without my sister being able to grasp me, words, which I didn't understand, continued to whirl around in my mind. I cried bitterly then and thought I should not receive Communion until I had confessed. My sister tried hard to soothe me, but as my tears continued to flow she offered to go and speak to Fr Pinho, who was preaching in a nearby parish.

Not daring to tell Deolinda all that was happening inside me, I asked her for a postcard with a picture of Our Lady on it, and I wrote him an account of what was happening. I placed this under my pillow until Deolinda was ready to leave. Suddenly Fr Pinho arrived with a seminarian. He had come to bring me Holy Communion as he knew that the parish priest was absent. When he told me that he had Jesus with him, I explained at once that I could not receive him without confession, but my tears and shame prevented me from adding anything else. Finally, after much effort, I managed to tell him that I had written the postcard. He took it and read it and understood everything. He tried to calm me then, affirming that he had foreseen all this, but had felt it prudent not to mention it to me.

This tribulation was repeated many times in an even more violent manner. My body became covered with purple bruises from the blows I received. . . . My one consolation was that the many people who came to assist me in these attacks were given such dramatic proof of the existence of Hell that they would surely not offend Our Lord any more."

Fr Pinho graphically describes the assaults as follows:

For a long time the demon tormented Alexandrina in various ways but he never touched her physically. Having threatened to ruin her, he launched the most furious attacks against her. There was scarcely an hour of the day when she did not feel persecuted by him. The worst moments occurred from midday until three in the afternoon (while she was praying for priests), and after nine in the evening (when she was praying for those sinning against purity). At these times, she not only had diabolical obsession, but even moments of true possession. During her violent struggles with the fiend, this paralysed woman with no strength and a weight of only 33 kilos, tried very violently to hurl herself against the irons of the bed and bite herself, so that not even four people could hold her down completely. On 7 October 1937, the devil made her swear and utter unseemly words, of whose meaning she was totally ignorant.

When in the name of God Fr Pinho demanded the identity of her invisible assailant, everyone in the quivering room heard the fearful reply. "I am Satan. Do not doubt that it is I." The devil cursed the priest and threatened to tear him to pieces.

Tearfully, Alexandrina begged Our Lord to intervene and end the attacks. Gently and compassionately, he explained how he needed this further suffering of hers to help more sinners. He reputedly told her in a number of ecstasies:

My daughter, suffering is the key to Heaven. I have endured so much to open Heaven to all mankind, but for many it was in vain. They say "I want to enjoy life, I have come into the world only for enjoyment." They say "Hell does not exist." I have died for them, and they say they did not ask me to do so. They have formed heresies against me. In order to save them, I select certain souls and lay the cross on their shoulders. Happy the soul who understands the value of suffering! My cross is sweet if carried for love of me. . . . I chose you from your mother's womb. I watch over you in your great difficulties. It was I who chose them for you, that I might have a victim to offer me much reparation. Lean on my Sacred Heart and find therein strength to suffer everything.

During the ecstasies, Our Lord went on to plead for Eucharistic reparation:

Keep me company in the Blessed Sacrament. I remain in the tabernacle night and day, waiting to give my love and grace to all who would visit me. But so few come. I am so abandoned, so lonely, so offended. . . . Pray for the unhappy sinners who, slaves of their passions, do not remember that they have a soul to save and that an eternity awaits them in a short while. . . . Many men do not believe in my existence; they do not believe that I live in the tabernacle. They curse me. Others believe, but do not love me and do not visit me; they live as if I were not there. I have chosen you to keep me company in those little refuges. Many of them are so wretched, but what riches inside! . . . Like Mary Magdalene, you have chosen the better part. You have chosen to love me in the tabernacles where you can contemplate me, not with the eyes of the body, but with those of the soul. I am truly present there as in Heaven – Body, Blood, Soul and Divinity. You have chosen that which is most sublime.

One day Fr Pinho celebrated Mass in the little room with the intention that God would release Alexandrina from the diabolical attacks. He said nothing to the seer about his prayer but immediately Mass was over she told him that God could not grant what he had asked for. "And what did I ask from Our Lord?" the priest enquired. "That he would free me from these attacks of the devil," she replied. Astonished, Fr Pinho responded, "And would you not wish to have this grace and receive other sufferings in their place?" The sick woman shook her head. "No, father. Pray rather that I do the Will of God in everything."

On one occasion, shaken witnesses claimed to have seen Alexandrina's bed enveloped in black, billowing smoke from which issued an insufferable stench. When Fr Pinho questioned them about it, they were willing to swear to the truth of their story.

Years later when Fr Pasquale SDB became her spiritual director, he gave Deolinda authority to order the devil to retreat, using holy water at the same time. By this means, Alexandrina was frequently freed from the attacks almost instantaneously.

After some ten years of unremitting savagery, the devil finally abandoned her and acted only on her imagination in the distance, as if he were chained down and threshing about in impotent rage, unable or forbidden to reach her again.

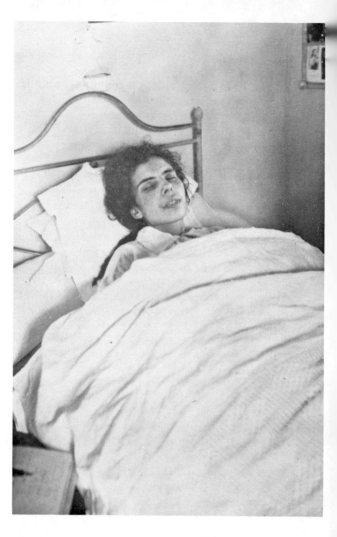

Alexandrina in ecstasy. This picture was taken in 1937 when Alexandrina was thirty-three years old.

5

Ecstasies of the Passion

The sublime vision of Our Lord which Alexandrina had reputedly seen on 6 September 1934 marked the beginning of a series of revelations in which Jesus reportedly instructed the seer step by step in the sorrows of his life and Passion. She had repeated revelations on the eternal loss of many souls and the crimes of peoples and nations blinded by sin. To a world plunging down the broad road to perdition, Our Lord seemed to be crying out in anguish: "Implore pardon . . . do what you preach! I am very much offended. . . . What dreadful criminals populate Hell! I warned Sodom and Gomorrha, but it had no effect. Unhappy ones . . . the same punishment will be meted out to you."

At these words, Alexandrina would turn pale and multiply her offerings in an attempt to hold back the arm of divine justice from punishing mankind with a second world war. She was given to understand that the war could only be averted by the consecration of the world to the Immaculate Heart of Mary. To obtain this unprecedented grace, Alexandrina offered herself anew as a victim for peace. Our Lord welcomed her prayer and again promised to give her his sorrowful Passion as a sign that the consecration would ultimately be effected and the days of tribulation shortened.

During this period Alexandrina entered into the phase of obscure contemplation. She recalled in her autobiography:

> If Jesus increased his graces and favours towards me, at the same time my doubts multiplied and the fear of deceiving myself and those who lived with me continually grew. . . . It seemed to me that they were all false and of

my own invention. My God, what torment! The darkness closed on me and there was no one to show me the way. However hard my spiritual director worked to inculcate confidence in me, there was nothing that served to comfort me.*

Despite her distress, the revelations continued. There were awful disclosures on the state of perdition of many souls. She seemed to hear Our Lord say:

Every moment countless sinners are provoking the wrath of God on the world − the most tremendous wrath. Unhappy ones if they are not converted! Poor world, whatever will become of it! Penitence, penitence throughout the world! Penitence! Oh world, acknowledge your crimes or you will be destroyed! Woe to the world! Divine Justice cannot support it any more.

The warnings were followed by searing visions of World War II.

In a spate of tears, Alexandrina cried out, "O my Jesus, I want to suffer all! I want to be crushed by you! I am your victim . . . but do not punish the world. I wish to be the lightning conductor of your wrath." At the same time, she felt the acute need to fortify her soul for the awesome trials which she instinctively knew lay ahead. She asked for and was able to make a retreat under the direction of Fr Pinho. She wrote of this period:

For a long time I was feeling great agony in my soul, and often seemed to be on the brink of falling into the fearful abyss. But in the days of my retreat, my suffering redoubled. The abyss opened to threaten me. The Justice of the Eternal Father was falling on me crying out, "Vengeance! . . . Vengeance! . . ." increasing my sorrows

*Readers unfamiliar with ascetic and mystic ways could be misled by these reservations of the Servant of God. They are however, an evident sign that the communication between God and Alexandrina was probably genuine. If she were too sure of herself we should be more distrustful. Cf. *Memoirs and Letters of Sister Lucia*, Professor A. Martins, SJ, 1973, page 417 footnote.

of soul and body. It is impossible to describe them; only one who has felt and seen them can understand. At the terrible voice of the Eternal Father, I spent days and nights tossing and turning in bed.

She continues:

On the morning of 2 October 1938, Our Lord told me that I would have to pass through all of his Passion from Gethsemane to Calvary, but that I would not arrive at the *Consummatum Est.* He confirmed that I would begin on the following day and that I would repeat these sufferings every Friday immediately after midday, until three o'clock in the afternoon. I did not say no to the Lord. I warned my spiritual director of everything and waited anxiously for the morrow because neither of us could imagine what was going to happen. During the night of 2-3 October, my agony of soul was intense, but the suffering of my body was even greater. I began to lose blood and felt fearful pains. And it was in this suffering that I entered into my first crucifixion. That horror I felt deep inside. Oh, how unspeakable were my afflictions!

Each ecstasy of the Passion (she had some 180 of them) was preceded by many hours of increasing dread which became overwhelming as midday Friday approached. The fear was often accompanied by an immense sadness, nausea, and a sensation of terrifying isolation. The times given here are Portuguese, one hour ahead of Greenwich Mean Time.

The frightful experience scarred Alexandrina's memory. Seven years later she was still living in her mind that first crucifixion. "Everything seemed to be present to me", she wrote. "I felt the fear and horror of those bitter hours, the anxiety of my spiritual director beside me, and the tears of my family who were terrified and weeping."

Shortly after midday on 3 October 1938, Our Lord invited her to undergo his Passion. "See, my daughter, Calvary is ready. Do you accept?" Alexandrina bravely consented. Awed witnesses held their breath as she entered into ecstasy and recovering the use of her paralysed limbs, almost levitated from the bed and underwent the agonising motions of Gethsemane to Calvary. The Passion ecstasies were filmed and the pictures form an important part of the deposition of her cause for beatification in Rome.

An eyewitness, Signorina Concetta, who taught in the village school, has left a vivid account of one of these extra-ordinary ecstasies.

> At the hour fixed by Jesus, our "seraph of love" began to suffer for us and for many sinners whom she wanted to save. I assisted at that agony, but I do not know how to describe it. She suffered from the Garden to the Cross. Oh how everything was reproduced in that frail body of Alexandrina!
>
> When Jesus told her that the hour was drawing near, that everything was prepared for her *via dolorosa*, step by step, as far as Calvary, she replied very courageously, "Yes Jesus, for you and to save sinners, I will do everything." It was then that she suffered the agony, the scourging, the crowning with thorns, the prison and the meeting with Our Lady at whom she gazed with a sorrow such as my eyes have never before seen.
>
> The falls under the cross were so visible that they left no room for any doubt. . . . In my opinion, her agony intensified when she presented her little white hands and then her feet to be nailed. Then the cross was fixed in the earth . . . what a heart-rending scene! What sadness flooded our souls! There followed the agony on the cross with her sad and penetrating groans. And her gaze! It was indescribable! She sighed repeatedly and in the end, closed her hollow eyes in the violet sockets, bent her head and died. What a faithful copy of the death of Jesus!

After the first Passion ecstasy, Fr Pinho requested Alexandrina not to leave her bed again, but Our Lord insisted to the seer that she should be left alone and the priest subsequently withdrew his order.

When the ecstasy ended at 3.00 p.m. Alexandrina raised her hands as if in thanksgiving, then suddenly gasped in horror. She cried:

No Jesus! No Jesus! Crucify me! Pardon! Pardon! Pardon! They have the same right as I have, because you died on the cross for them as well as for me. Jesus, I want no soul to go to Hell, neither in my parish nor in the entire world. I love you for them. Forget the sinners, Jesus. Remember me through my crucifixion. Hell is the most terrifying inferno, Jesus. [This dialogue bears a striking resemblance to what took place between Our Lord and the mystic St Gemma Galgani at the end of the nineteenth century.]

A few days later Alexandrina felt atrocious pains. She began to vomit blood and was tortured by a thirst of such burning intensity that water was useless; she was unable to swallow a drop. At the same time, she was overcome by the appalling "smell of sin". "I began to smell odours incredibly repugnant", she recalled in her autobiography. "They bought me violets and perfumes to hold to my nose, but I pushed them away because I was still tormented by the same vile smell. Just the memory of these things makes me suffer."

With the onset of the second Passion ecstasy, Fr Pinho felt it prudent to keep the mysterious trances secret. For three years only a select number of people were aware of them. In 1941 however, a visiting missionary (Fr Terça, of the Missionaries of the Holy Spirit) witnessed one of them and wrote an account of it in a popular Portuguese magazine. The publication caused Alexandrina much suffering as it made her a focus of attention. Thousands from all over the country thronged to see the "Victim of Balasar", as she became widely known. Besides its untimely publication, the article contained several minor inaccuracies which gave rise to erroneous interpretations in the medical and scientific fields. The narrative had, however, much value for its vivid description and accurate chronological sequence. It reads as follows:

"On 29 August 1941, I entered the room accompanied by four other priests with the necessary authority. It was just 1.00 p.m. I went across to the bed of the sick woman and saw in her eyes the signs of a deep sadness. I asked, 'Alexandrina, how do you feel?' 'I am afraid', she replied with a voice full of bitterness. . . . 'The hour is approaching.' The light in her eyes faded and at eight minutes past one she closed her eyelids. She had entered into ecstasy.

A few minutes after 1.10 p.m. she became agitated; still on the bed, she stretched out her left hand and made a light gesture as if to ward off an approaching enemy.

1.12 p.m. She groans many times in distress. Then turning towards the floor of the room, she frees herself from the bedcovering almost in levitation and falling on her knees with a rapid movement, remains face down on the floor.* The left hand stretches out while with the right hand, she attempts to hide her face which is tortured and afflicted.

1.14 p.m. She leans on her elbows, hides her face with her hands and emits anguished sighs.

1.15 p.m. She is seized by an indescribable distress. She rolls on the ground, remaining in the position in which St Cecilia was found in the catacombs, her face above her joined hands.

1.16 p.m. Light movement of the arms, a sigh of affliction. She presses her face between her hands and one hears acute groans. The breathing is slow and deep.

1.18 p.m. She extends her arms in the attitude of one who tries to repel an assailant. Again she turns on one side and crosses and clasps her fingers with distress.

1.20 p.m. More pronounced groans. She rolls twice along the bed. Her distress seems to be increased at seeing the suffering of Jesus in the Garden. Greatly afflicted, she rolls again in the direction of the wall, like a worm. Five times

---

*Alexandrina was in uninterrupted ecstasy for three and a half hours during the Passion ecstasies. She did not see or hear, but only contemplated the Passion of Jesus. At the same time she obeyed her spiritual director or his delegate and responded not only to explicit orders, but even to those given mentally.

the sorrowful groans are accompanied by painful muscular contractions.

1.25 p.m. Alexandrina kneels down and then takes a sitting position, supporting herself on her feet, but always with tormented distress. Then she rises, turns towards the door of the room and exclaims bitterly, "Could you not watch one hour with me? Watch and pray that you enter not into temptation."

1.28 p.m. The seer raises her arms high, then folds them in a cross. She falls again on her knees, and then face down with the elbows somewhat separated and the face between her hands.

1.29 p.m. She rolls painfully towards the right and groans. She raises her hand a little, then lets it fall on the floor beside the mat. [Deolinda attempted to mitigate the pains of these falls by spreading a mat on the floor in advance. At the spot where Alexandrina would rest her head, Deolinda placed a pillow.]

1.32 p.m. With unspeakable suffering, she makes two turns towards the left, remaining face down.

1.34 p.m. She assists at the struggle of Jesus with the temptor and suffers the sorrows of the Saviour. Her face appears inflamed and after two series of contractions, as if trembling with fear, she falls prostrate to the ground, striking her head beside the mat.*

1.38 p.m. She kneels down with pain. She rises, goes to sit near the bed and repeats the words of the Saviour, "Watch and pray, the hour is at hand." She raises her hands high

---

*Her doctor, Dr Azevedo, was most attentive. He took notes of everything that happened during the ecstasies. Other doctors sent by the ecclesiastical authorities to discover if there was any fraud or the existence of natural forces, examined the seer many times and violently goaded her while she was suffering in ecstasy. There was never once the slightest reaction from her. The unanimous verdict of the priests and doctors was that the phenomenon was inexplicable.

Alexandrina during one of the more than 180 Passion ecstasies which she experienced. She accepted Our Lord's invitation to relive His Passion. Alexandrina suffered intensely during these ecstasies; in this scene, she is brought before Pilate's tribunal.

Alexandrina during a Passion ecstasy—the scourging. During these ecstasies Alexandrina recovered the use of her paralyzed limbs. Those present witnessed the violent physical contractions she experienced during this torture. Alexandrina repeated the words of Jesus: "Father, this is for You, and to give You souls."

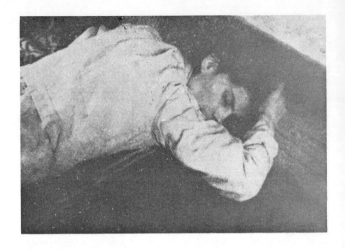

Alexandrina falling under the weight of the cross during a Passion ecstasy. As the soldiers dragged Jesus with ropes, Alexandrina was also dragged across the floor, face down, until she took up the cross again.

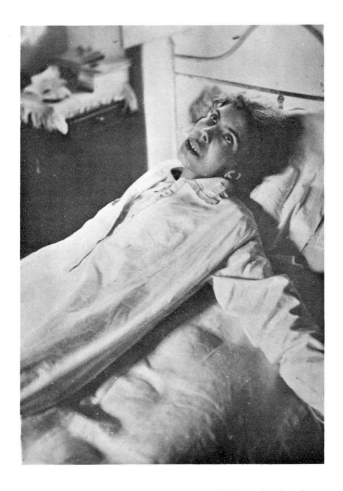

Alexandrina during a Passion ecstasy—"Father, forgive them, for they know not what they do!"

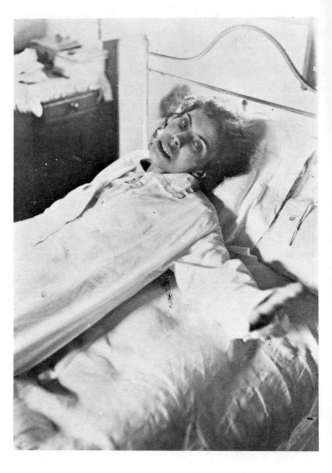

A scene during a Passion ecstasy—"Son, behold thy Mother."

After suffering the Passion of Our Lord, Alexandrina turns toward the parish church and speaks to Jesus Crucified.

Dr. Azevedo, who was Alexandrina's physician from 1941 until her death in 1955.

and says the words of Jesus, "My Father, sacrifice me, but save the world, the world which is yours."

1.43 p.m. She rises, goes a step forward and kneels down, then falls to the ground, moaning sorrowfully. She turns her face towards the left as if fearing a second assault from the enemy and still moaning, hides her face with her hands.

1.50 p.m. Prostrate on the ground, she rolls twice towards the bed and lets her head fall on the floor.

1.53 p.m. Oppressed by atrocious suffering, she rolls again, but towards the left, remaining face down and with the right arm extended on the mat.

1.54 p.m. She continues to groan painfully and leaning on her elbows, supports her head between her hands and contemplates Jesus in his agony in the Garden of Gethsemane.

1.55 p.m. She rolls again towards the door and extending her elbows, leans her head on the floor. She remains silent for a little while.

1.59 p.m. She emits more tortured groans and is agitated from head to foot by the violence of the torments. Then comes a period of quiet rest.

2.02 p.m. Grievously afflicted, she lets her head fall on the floor twice and sighs with intense agony. Between the groans, she remains sitting on the floor, but near the bed.

2.04 p.m. Raising her hands to Heaven, she repeats the words which were pronounced by Jesus, "My Father, I want to save the world; sacrifice me now. I want to give my life for men. Do not spare me from the sacrifice."

At this point, Alexandrina crosses her hands on her breast, and bends forward as if to see more clearly what is happening in the gloom. In the distance she sees soldiers with Judas at the head of them and she calls the apostles. Then she sits on the side of the bed where she rests for a while. Suddenly, she raises her left hand in an attitude of repulsion and hearing the soldiers approaching, she exclaims to the disciples, "Get up, the hour has come. Come, let us go."

2.06 p.m. She says the words of Judas, "Hail, Master." She feels with repugnance the kiss of the traitor. After several moments, she makes a sign with her left hand to the soldiers who had fallen to the ground. But seeing the Lord imprisoned, she also offers her hands to receive the fetters.

When Jesus is conducted to the house of Annas, he exclaims, "They have all abandoned me, even those who were my friends." Alexandrina repeats these words with an expression of intense bitterness. When the Saviour is dragged from one place to another, the seer, following his steps, makes several turns in the room on her knees with much weariness. Referring to Annas, Alexandrina paints a moral picture of him saying, "He is a cunning, arrogant old man. He is the same man who was confused many times when Jesus was preaching in the Temple."

2.10 p.m. Jesus is before the tribunal. Alexandrina, seated on the floor, takes the attitude of one who listens attentively and repeats the words of the Saviour, "I have taught in the synagogue and in the Temple. Why do you interrogate me? Question those who heard what I taught."

2.12 p.m. When the soldier says, "Is that the way you reply to the High Priest?" Alexandrina, getting up, gives herself a violent slap on her left cheek with her right hand. One of those present murmurs, "In truth, it was with the right hand that the soldier slapped Christ and on the left cheek that Jesus felt the blow."

2.13 p.m. While Jesus is conducted to the tribunal of Caiphas, he meets Peter and says to him, "Peter, you have sworn fidelity to me. You were the most loved disciple, the friend of my heart."

In the tribunal, after being insidiously questioned by Caiphas, Jesus says, "How far you are from seeing the light!" Alexandrina repeats these words of the Saviour and the preceding ones, seated on the floor and facing the west, as one who is observing everything from a distance.

Thwarted and wearied by the lack of proof against Jesus, Caiphas turns to his colleagues in the tribunal and exclaims, "We must deal with this man as soon as possible." It was then that he asked Jesus this question: "Are you the Christ, the Son of God?" "You have said it", Jesus replied.

From the house of Caiphas Jesus is brought to the tribunal of Pilate, and from there to the house of Herod. This journey is followed by the seer who drags herself on her knees across the room. On the return from Herod to the tribunal of Pilate, Alexandrina repeats the following reflection of the Saviour: "To be treated like a madman is of little importance if I have souls to save."

In the tribunal of Pilate, the seer repeats the words of the multitude and among others, the following: "Crucify him! Crucify him!" And those of Claudia, the wife of the Governor: "Have nothing to do with this just man."

2.24 p.m. When Jesus is led to the column, Alexandrina moves towards the bed and there leans on her hands. At the sight of Jesus being scourged, she receives on herself the quivering blows against the Lord and from the violent contractions produced by the whips and the anguished groans that escape her lips, one can infer how much she is suffering.* The second group of soldiers come to relieve the first who are tired of hurling blows on their victim. The scourging of Jesus, already horribly tortured, strikes the poor martyr as well. During these torments, Alexandrina, who impersonates the Saviour, raises her eyes to Heaven and exclaims, "For love of you, O Father, I want and embrace your cross." One then hears anguished groans from

*The punishment of scourging normally preceded the execution of a condemned man. Alexandrina later described the instruments of the scourging of Christ very precisely to Fr Pasquale, SDB. The back, the breast, the stomach and the face of the condemned man, she disclosed, were struck at will by the soldiers.

the lips of Alexandrina, and she repeats the words of the Saviour, "Father, this is for you, and to give you souls."

The blows of the whips on the body of the Lord rebound on the seer, forcing her to twist herself and to moan in a heart-rending manner. Jesus exclaims through her mouth, "For you, O Father. . . . It is for your love!"

2.32 p.m. Alexandrina falls on her knees with her face resting on the bed. She groans again, with painful contractions on account of her unspeakable torture.

2.36 p.m. The Lord is again scourged and the seer is again martyred.

2.38 p.m. She repeats the words which she hears from the Saviour, "Father, it is for you and for souls." She rises, falls on her knees again near the bed, almost exhausted by the violence of the torments. At last she takes a brief rest on the bed.

2.39 p.m. The scourging of the Lord continues and she suffers violent contractions again all over her frail body and finally falls to the ground exhausted. Soon, however, she gets up, and very tired sits on the floor between her sister and the bed on which she leans. Raising her eyes to Heaven she repeats the words of Jesus, "My Father, my Father, who will not love you?" In this manner the scourging of the shoulders ends. Alexandrina moves to the head of the bed and leaning on it, rests her face on the back of her right hand. She does not suffer; it is a relief that Jesus gives her to enable her to bear the remainder of the Passion. (She affirmed that sometimes Our Lady appeared to her at this juncture.) Finally Jesus is untied from the pillar and re-tied so that he can be scourged on the breast.

2.41 p.m. There are other scourgings, and while the blows fall on the Lord, she has violent contractions, so great are the wounds which reach her from Jesus.

2.44 p.m. The last scourging ends; she falls prostrate on the floor with her head resting on the bed.

2.45 p.m. To accompany the Lord towards the place of the crowning, Alexandrina moves to the wall of the room on her knees and sits down. She participates in the torments of the Lord, receiving in a mysterious manner the crown of thorns. She suffers and moans painfully with Jesus. Her head trembles with the sharpness of the pains produced by the thorns driven into the head of the Saviour. This torture lasts for 28 minutes. [Alexandrina later explained to Fr Pasquale SDB that it was not just a crown around the head, it was a helmet of thorns which covered all the head. She added that Our Lord's face closely resembled that on the Shroud of Turin.]

3.13 p.m. While they place the wood of the cross on the shoulders of Jesus, Alexandrina hears these words of the Saviour when he stands before the Roman governor. "Pilate, I will have compassion for the weakness of your soul." Then, on her knees, she goes to the door of the room and sits down.

3.21 p.m. Alexandrina carries the cross on her shoulders and follows the Saviour on her knees.*

3.25 p.m. Alexandrina follows Jesus in the first fall and her head strikes the floor. When the soldiers drag Jesus with the ropes, Alexandrina is also dragged across the floor, face down, until she takes the cross again.

---

*At this moment, while the seer was carrying the cross to Calvary, Dr Azevedo invited one of the priests present to try to lift the seer from the floor. The strongest priest was chosen. He took her by her armpits and strained his utmost, but was unable to move her. She then weighed only 40 kilos. One day, the renowned psychiatrist Dr E. de Moura was present. Removing his jacket he took Alexandrina under the armpits in a brusque manner and exerting all his strength, tried to lift her. He could not displace her by one centimetre. A sudden movement of the seer then sent him reeling back with his legs in the air. During the ascent to Calvary, Fr Pinho remembered one time when he asked Alexandrina if she could tell him the weight of the cross. Still in ecstasy, she replied that it had the weight of the whole world. "A profound theological reply", commented Fr Pasquale later.

3.28 p.m. At the second fall of the Saviour, Alexandrina
also falls, receiving a painful bruise on her forehead. She is
then dragged to the door of the room to take up the share
of the cross again which the Heavenly Bridegroom gives her.
Jesus resumes the walk of the execution and meets his holy
Mother. Alexandrina repeats his words, "My Mother, my
Heart is united with yours." The look of compassion which
the seer gives when she sees the face of the Holy Virgin is
infinitely touching. Mary meets her Divine Son, almost
fainting, without support or comfort.

3.31 p.m. Alexandrina suffers a new torture in the arms and
head when she falls again on the floor. After the third fall,
Simon of Cyrene is obliged to carry the cross.[1] The Saviour
was barefoot and walking along stony ground. The violent
wrenching of the ropes, together with his physical exhaustion, made him stumble and fall.

Seeing Jesus reach Calvary and being stripped of his garments, Alexandrina mimes the scene expressively and after
kneeling down, fixes the cross and stretches herself on it.
She then presents her right hand to be nailed to the wood
and then the left hand and the feet, suffering excruciating
tortures.[2] While she is on the cross, the High Priest and the
people swear at Jesus, saying, "If you are the king of the
Jews, come down from that cross!" Jesus then says the
following words which the seer repeats with gentle grief:

---

1. The priest mentioned in the note above was again invited by the
doctor to try and raise the seer, who was dragging herself along on
her knees. He succeeded without any effort. The explanation is
patent: the first time there was also the weight of the cross.

2. Fr Pasquale asked Alexandrina why she painfully stretched her
fingers to touch her wrists and not the palms of her hands. She
replied, "Because Our Lord was nailed on the wrists, not the hands."
It was found impossible to detach her arm from the floor after she
had been nailed to the cross. Another detail worthy of note: just as
she was nailed, she turned over for a few seconds and then took a
supine position again. When asked the reason for this she explained,
"Because at that moment they turned over the cross of Jesus, to
beat the nails in further."

"Father, forgive them, for they know not what they do."
Since the bad thief was swearing, the good thief made
himself the advocate of the Lord saying, "We are being
punished for our crimes, but this man has not harmed
anyone." Alexandrina then repeats these words of Jesus
to the good thief, "In truth I say to you, this day you will
be with me in Paradise." Raising her eyes to Heaven the
seer continues to repeat what she hears from the mouth of
Our Lord regarding the good thief: "Father, I wish that
where I am he may also be, and that my reign may be your
reign."

3.37 p.m. With atrocious suffering, Alexandrina continues
to be stretched on the floor with her arms open, nailed to
that mysterious cross. Repeatedly she groans in agony.
Then staring fixedly at someone whom she loves much she
says, "Woman, behold your son." And then to John,
"Behold your Mother."

3.40 p.m. She gives a painful and prolonged groan and
exclaims with indescribable bitterness, "My Father, why
have you forsaken me?" She breathes deeply and groans,
then remains silent for some while. The breast of
Alexandrina expands in anguish and it seems that the
breathing is paralysed.

3.50 p.m. Soon after she groans again. Her cries are so
moving and soul-stirring that they can never be forgotten.
Then the tortured woman exclaims, "All is consummated."
The breathing remains suspended for some seconds and
finally, the breast is expanded in the struggle of death. One
hears prolonged cries of anguish. It is the last agony. With a
feeble voice she utters the last sad groans and exclaims,
"Father, into your hands I commend my spirit." Her head
falls gently on the left side. To the eyes of a watcher,
Alexandrina is dead. Not a movement, not a sign of breathing. She is dead — or seems to be dead, and remains so for
about thirty seconds."

Thus ends the eyewitness account of one of these his-
torically unprecedented ecstasies. Those privileged to
witness them were overwhelmed with emotion, feeling
themselves at the very gates of Jerusalem and seeing the
Passion of Jesus. The contusions caused by Alexandrina's
falls and the purple bruises visible on many parts of her
body disappeared in a short time. It is significant that, out
of humility, Alexandrina prayed to Our Lord not to give her
the stigmata or any other visible signs of her mysterious
sufferings.

During the early months of 1942, her little room was
besieged daily by crowds of pilgrims. Though her suffering
between each Passion ecstasy was severe and continuous,
she never tired urging frequent Communion and the devout
daily recitation of the rosary as the cure for the world's ills.
Penance was her constant refrain, and she repeatedly
advocated consecration to the Immaculate Heart of Mary
through the Brown Scapular of Our Lady of Mount Carmel
whose picture hung above her bed. To her left hung another
picture of little Jacinta Marto, the youngest of the three
children who saw Our Lady at Fatima in 1917. Frequently
she would draw attention to this picture and urge that
Jacinta's heroic example of sacrifice be imitated.

As for sin, Alexandrina would plead in a heartbreaking
voice for its permanent renouncement, cost what it might
in prayer and mortification. To offend God, she stressed to
the pilgrims, was the supreme evil in life and the most
resolute personal efforts must be made towards its total
elimination. "O sinners," she would weep, "I am enduring a
life of terrible suffering on your behalf. Convert yourselves!
Sin no more! Sin no more!" Great numbers responded, as
indicated by the long queues at the confessional in the
village church. "Your house", Our Lord told her, "has
become the Calvary of sinners."

6

The Eucharist alone

During Holy Week of 1942, Alexandrina's condition deteriorated alarmingly. Her interminable pain, shot through with acute spasms of nausea, grew so agonising that it seemed her chalice of sorrow would overflow and her martyred soul take its flight to eternity. Despite a ravenous hunger and burning thirst, she was unable to retain any nourishment except a little milk and mineral water. On Palm Sunday evening she asked to be anointed, fearing that she would lose consciousness before receiving the sacrament As soon as it had been administered she stammered, "I am so happy now. All my faults have been removed."

By Maundy Thursday her agony was almost unendurable. When Deolinda touched her burning lips with a glass of water, Alexandrina gasped, "O my God! My thirst can only be satisfied by you! On earth there is no remedy." Hour after fiery hour her frightful torment continued. "Oh what nausea!" she groaned. "It is really of the damned in Hell. It cannot be but the fruit of sin." As the evening closed in, she rallied slightly and murmured that she did not have the usual fear of the Friday Passion. When asked the reason she confided, "I do not know how it is, but I feel certain that Our Lord will not give it to me."

She was right. And a great sigh of joy escaped her as she realised that the consecration of the world to the Immaculate Heart of Mary had been decided on. Early on Good Friday morning she heard Jesus announce to her in a tone of triumph, "Glory to Mary! The world will be consecrated to her. It belongs to Jesus and to the Mother of Jesus." [The consecration was effected by Pope Pius XII on 31 October 1942, using the very titles that had been revealed to

Alexandrina: "Queen of the Universe, Queen of the Most Holy Rosary, Refuge of the human race, Victress in all God's battles." Days later came the "turning point" of the war, according to Sir Winston Churchill.]

In a blaze of agony and adoring love, Alexandrina cried out to Jesus in the tabernacle of the nearby church, "O my Eucharistic Love, I cannot live without you! O Jesus, transform me into your Eucharist! Mother, my dearest Mother, I wish to be of Jesus, I wish to be entirely yours!"

Deep in her soul she heard his profound reply:

> You will not take food again on earth. Your food will be my Flesh; your blood will be my Divine Blood, your life will be my Life. You receive it from me when I unite my Heart to your heart. Do not fear, my daughter. You will not be crucified any more as in the past. . . . And now a new trial awaits you, which will be the most painful of all.* But in the end I will carry you to Heaven and the Holy Mother will accompany you.

And so it was on Good Friday 1942 that Alexandrina began an absolute fast which was to last more than thirteen years until her death, her sole nourishment being Holy Communion which she received with moving devotion every morning. Meanwhile, her agonising pain continued without respite. "My body seems to have no bones", she panted. "It seems a pulp. I am like a statue of chalk which must not be touched or it will crumble."

Her family and friends, believing her to be dying, never left her sick-bed; not could they explain an existence which was only pain. Visions of the Holy Family and her guardian angel gave her fleeting relief from her appalling suffering. But as the days without nourishment lengthened into weeks and months, the suspense of her watchful family steadily grew.

Alexandrina became convinced that the end was near. "O Our Lady!" she wept, "Come to take me! I cannot bear

---

*The last Passion ecstasy occurred on 27 March 1942 which was then the feast of Our Lady of Sorrows.

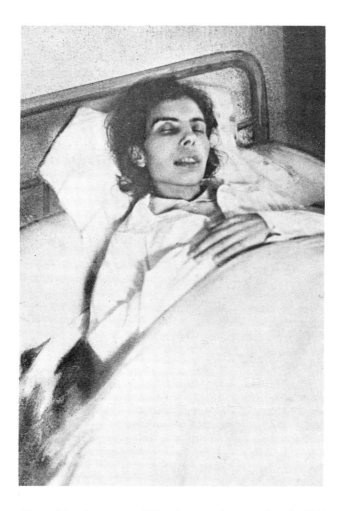

Alexandrina in ecstasy. This photograph was taken in 1941 when Alexandrina was thirty-seven. The following year, on Good Friday of 1942, she began an absolute fast which was to last more than thirteen years, until her death. Her only nourishment was daily Communion.

this suffering any more . . . O Jesus, my love, do not abandon the one who loves you so much! O days which never end! O Heaven which never approaches!" Turning to her relatives she groaned, "When you hear the bells sound for my death, go down on your knees, pray and thank Jesus and Our Lady for coming to take me."

Every Friday, she felt a wave of nostalgia for the Passion she had suffered for the last four years. "One esteems something only when one has lost it", she sighed. "If I had the Passion now, I would embrace it with an eternal embrace and would never separate myself from it." To ease her yearning, she had brought to her the long gown which she had worn during the Passion ecstasies. She would gaze at it with a faraway look and then tearfully embrace it. At other times, she would reverently kiss the large mat on which took place the successive stations of her mysterious martyrdom.

Her longing for that mystical Calvary was only tempered by her greater longing for death. She begged God to take her on the first Friday of May, to enable her to celebrate in heaven the first Saturday she loved so much. But the first week in May passed and her agony continued to rack her day and night without respite. On 24 May, feast of Our Lady Help of Christians, after almost two months of absolute fasting "with a burning thirst and a longing for food", Alexandrina cried out in anguish, "I sigh, I die, I long to satisfy my soul with the food of Paradise!"

As the months passed, news of Alexandrina's fast spread far and wide. Crowds of pilgrims again besieged her sick-room, imploring her prayers and favours. Their endless importunity seemed to heighten her ferocious suffering, but panting on her bed of pain she promised to remember everyone in her prayers. Of this period she wrote later:

Day by day, moment by moment, my life became more and more painful. On the one hand, obedience obliges me to live hidden and to receive people in such a way as to be soon forgotten. O my God, if I had my will that is how I would live. But what deceit! The more I want to

be hidden, the more they make me known. Visitors
arrive from everywhere — what torment for me.

One afternoon, a number of important-looking men
entered the sickroom to investigate reports of Alexandrina's
total fast. She relates the event as follows:

At half past two in the afternoon, five men entered the
room. At once I had a presentiment that one of them
was a doctor. They began to question me. For some
reason, I found my attention drawn to one of them and
after they had gone, I knew instinctively that he was a
doctor. I answered their questions calmly and firmly, for
truth has only one reply. When they asked me incredul-
ously if it was true that I ate and drank nothing, not
knowing whether they were believers or not, I answered:
"I receive Holy Communion every day." They remained
silent and non-committal for a while and shortly afterwards they respectfully withdrew.

Not everyone, however, treated Alexandrina with the
same courtesy. Doubts and suspicions about her fast
circulated; some openly accused Deolinda and her mother
of perpetrating a monstrous fraud. These accusations, and
the indignation of many zealous people, were the cause of
much sorrow for Alexandrina and her family. Finally, her
friends appealed to the medical authorities to intervene and
establish the authenticity of the prodigy once and for all.

Alexandrina vividly describes all that followed. She
wrote on 27 May 1943: "In order to satisfy the desires and
the will of the Archbishop, I subjected myself once more to
a medical examination. When they told me about this, a
new suffering took possession of my spirit, but seeing in
everything the holy Will of God, I accepted, as always
through obedience. When they told me the day on which
the doctors would come, I prayed with great fervour to Our
Lady to give me the necessary composure to bear everything with courage and resignation for Jesus and for souls.

"On the appointed day, the doctor in attendance came
to our house with Dr Enrico Gomes di Araujo and Dr Carlo

Lima. Fortunately I was calm and serene; God had heard my prayer. One of the doctors asked me if I suffered much and for whom I offered my sufferings. He also asked whether I suffered willingly and if I would be happy if God released me from my sorrows. I replied that, in truth, I suffered much and that I offered everything for the love of God and for the conversion of sinners.

"They then asked me what was my greatest aspiration and I answered, 'It is Heaven.' They then enquired if I wanted to be a saint like St Teresa or St Clare and to arrive in Heaven leaving behind a name famous throughout the world. 'I am not in the least interested in that', I replied. They then asked, 'If it were necessary to lose your soul to save sinners, what would you do?' I answered, 'I trust that I would also be saved, but if I had to lose my soul I would say no, because God would never ask such a thing.'

"'Why do you not eat?' they then asked. And I replied, 'I do not eat because I cannot. I feel full. I do not need it. However, I have a longing for food.'

"The doctors then began the examination which I bore with good disposition. At the end, seeing that I was in no condition to make a journey, they decided to call two nuns to verify the truth of my fast. After they left, I remained waiting for their decision. On 4 June my confessor came to give me Communion, accompanied by my doctor, who afterwards explained that I was being given the opportunity to enter a hospital in Oporto to have the fast medically certified. I would be isolated for a month and under constant observation. I immediately said 'No' – but at once I was sorry, thinking of the obedience I owed the Archbishop and the difficult situation of my spiritual director, my doctor and my relatives and friends. So I accepted the proposal, subject to three conditions – I would be able to receive Holy Communion every day, I would be accompanied by my sister, and I would not be subjected to any more medical examinations because I was only entering the hospital for observation.

"By 10 June all was ready for my journey to the hospital of Foce del Duro in Oporto. My grief was great, but I had such faith in Jesus that I felt he would, if necessary, send his angels to help me. When my doctor arrived, he hesitated for some while, as if loath to tell me I had to leave. Finally I managed to say, 'Let's go, doctor. He who does not leave does not return!'

"I embraced my family and friends and only Jesus knew the sorrow it cost me to separate myself from them. I looked only into his Sacred Heart and the Immaculate Heart of Mary, and implored them to give me courage and strength to bear this new affliction. As they levered my stretcher downstairs I murmured to my weeping family, 'Courage! All for Jesus and for souls!' I was unable to say more. There was such a tightening of my heart that I felt it would be impossible to keep back the tears.

"Over a hundred people were surrounding the ambulance. I saw tears in the eyes of almost all. The sorrow I felt then was indescribable. My heart was beating with such violence that it seemed about to burst my ribs. Inwardly I prayed, 'Accept these throbbings, my dear Jesus, for your love and for the salvation of souls.'

"The journey was difficult; it seemed to me that my heart would not hold out.* Every now and then, I looked at my sister and saw how desolate she was. By the grace of God, I was able to keep the smile on my lips. But the constant shaking of the ambulance was sheer torture and I prayed repeatedly, 'All for your love, my dear Jesus, and may the darkening of my spirit serve to give light to other spirits.'

"When we arrived at Matozinhos, the doctor raised the curtains so that I could look at the sea. An enormous silence filled my spirit, and observing the continuous movement of the waves, I asked Jesus to let my love beat like them without interruption."

---

*The road from Balasar to Povoa is still badly broken and rutted and the ambulance journey must have caused Alexandrina severe pain.

7

Medical confirmation

"At length we reached the hospital, but before they withdrew me from the ambulance, my face was covered with a cloth so that no one would recognise me. Going up the stairs was a martyrdom as they carried me up head down. When they reached a small room, my face was uncovered and I found myself surrounded by doctors and nurses. I was dismayed to discover that Deolinda had been allocated an adjoining room, contrary to what I had asked for. I did not know how I could manage without her experienced help and constant words of encouragement. Dr Araujo then arrived and began to give instructions to the nurses and assistants.

"After he had gone, my own doctor remained for some while and two nurses charged with watching all my movements took up their station by my bed. When Dr Azevedo finally left that evening, I could not restrain my tears any longer. For a long time I wept, offering my tears and grief to Jesus. On seeing me so desolate, the nurses permitted Deolinda to remain near me that night, together with another nurse who learned from her the correct way of turning me.

"The following day, a Friday, I began my true Calvary in that place. I had an ecstasy in the morning (I have one every Friday), and the doctors and nurses gathered round my bed. Dr Azevedo was there and after writing the words of the ecstasy he passed them round for the other doctors to read. Nothing escaped their watchful gaze, not even the most insignificant detail which was commented on at once. . . . Dr Araujo was very strict, even to the point of harshness. He sternly forbade any nurse to question me in the slightest way. When one of the nurses tried to comfort Deolinda, who was weeping because of my condition, Dr Araujo immediately dismissed her and forbade her to enter my room again.

"During the night of Friday to Saturday, I had a great crisis of vomiting which made me suffer severely and which was made worse by the absence of my sister who knew how to sustain me. Dr Araujo arrived in the morning, but my prostration was such that I did not hear him knock at the door. I heard him whisper to one of the nurses by my bed, 'It is all over with her.'

"At these words, I opened my eyes and said, 'Doctor, I have had these crises at home.' He replied curtly, 'Miss, don't think that you have come here to fast.' I understood what he meant and felt deeply wounded.

"When he was informed of the ecstasy of the previous day, he asked for the notes of it and having read them, commented, 'It seems impossible that Dr Azevedo, so intelligent, lets himself be deceived by these things. It is necessary to make an end of this nonsense. From now on, take away all the clocks so that the sick woman will be ignorant of the time.' (As if the Lord had need of clocks!)

"Dr Araujo then tried to treat me with medication, but I would not consent. Several times the nurse came near me, convinced that I was dead. For five days I underwent a continuous agony, more in the spirit than in the body, because in those crises, they never permitted Deolinda to come near me, while at home two people were frequently necessary to sustain me. All were persuaded that the crises were due to a lack of nourishment and they kept me isolated, convinced that I would ultimately be compelled to ask for food, or else die of starvation. How they deceived themselves! They did not know that nourishment came to me from the Sacred Host which I received every day.

"When Dr Azevedo returned and learnt of the attempts to make me take medicine and nourishment, he said to the hospital staff, 'This sick woman has only come so that the reality of her fast and the normality of her mental faculties can be ascertained – nothing more. I trust that Dr Araujo will abide by these terms. I do not permit anyone to give her injections or medication, unless she specifically requests them, or I consent to it. You will see that after each crisis she has, the dark rings under her eyes disappear, her colour returns and her pulse becomes normal.' He paused and then added, pointedly, 'I can assure you of one thing: without nourishment, you would die, I would die, but the sick woman here will not die.'

"His kind words on my behalf did much to rally my flagging spirits. Five days later, the vomiting stopped completely, the colour reappeared on my face and my pulse became normal.

"The strict surveillance by relays of doctors and nurses continued. Never for one moment was I left alone. The door of my room opened only to admit doctors and nurses. The improvement in my condition failed to convince any of them. They said it was impossible to live without nourishment and they tried to intimidate me, using soothing, persuasive tones to induce me to take food. But all their efforts were in vain. On one occasion I heard them affirm that my case could be one of hysteria, or a phenomenon still unknown to medical science.

"Dr Araujo visited me several times each day, occasionally taking me by surprise at night, as if to discover something. . . . Even if I live until the end of the world, I will never forget the apprehension I felt whenever he opened the door, and my anxious suspense of waiting for his words. So many times I prayed, 'May this night serve to give light to him, to the people who surround me and to all the souls who find themselves in darkness.'

"During his frequent interrogations of me, he tried in every possible way to persuade me to take food and end the fast. A nurse even tried, on many occasions, to take away my Faith. She used interminable arguments to discourage me and to convince me that what was happening to me was not the work of God. Once Dr Araujo said to me with a malicious expression, 'You convince yourself, Miss, that

God does not want you to suffer. If you wish to save souls, he can save them himself if it is true that he has the power to do so.' At other times when he questioned me, I seemed to see in front of me a wolf in sheep's clothing. I had the impression of seeing Satan himself trying to destroy my Faith and convince me that my immolation for souls was all an illusion.

"On one occasion I replied to him, 'The things of God are so great, so great, and we are so small, so small. At least, I am, doctor.' He stiffened and then said scornfully, 'You are right, but I am far greater than you – and by how much!' So saying, he took himself off.

"How far Dr Araujo was from comprehending this law of love for souls! If he knew the value of a soul, he would realise that everything is too small to save it. My stay in the hospital was a constant rain of humiliation and sacrifice. Oh, if I had known how to suffer for Jesus! To this end, I turned to little Jacinta of Fatima whose picture I keep at the foot of my bed, and said to her, 'Dear Jacinta, you who were so small have proved all this. You know how hard it is.' Only through prayer and the prayers of many good souls was I able to gain the strength to climb this sorrowful Calvary with such a heavy cross.

"One day, Dr Araujo sat down by my bed and tried to convince me that I was a victim of delusion. He began with an involved discourse on medicine and spoke of one of his professors to whom he had presented a long work, painstakingly put together during many days and nights of study. The professor read the work and asked him if he was certain that it was accurate. The doctor replied 'yes' and cited the arguments supporting his case. As the conversation lengthened, I looked at him, pretending that I did not understand, but thinking, 'You go so far to fall so near?' Meanwhile, the doctor continued, 'I was convinced that I had done a good job, but the professor let me finish and then, with a few deft strokes, briefly demolished my case. My breath was taken away. I felt humiliated over so many lost hours and the realisation that my long study had collapsed in a few seconds.' I had already guessed what was coming and replied, smiling, 'But my case does not fall, doctor. A very good and wise man follows me and has studied me for years. [Dr Azevedo.] If the work is of God, there is nothing that can make it collapse.' Dr Araujo seemed rather embarrassed and said, 'We will see,' and retired in a hurry.

"On the 17th and then on the 30th day of my stay at the hospital, my mother came to see me. I had such a desire to see her! But she stayed only a very short time and always under the watchful eye of the nurses who were keeping me under continual surveillance. When my mother wept, I had to smile and joke to conceal my sorrow.

"The difficult days passed with the endless changing of nurses under the directions of the doctor. With some, who went beyond the limits of their duties and their rights, I suffered more than with others. After some weeks, the doctor began to allow me a little freedom and permitted my sister to spend some time near me, though without giving her permission to touch me. On the 21st day, he allowed the nuns of the hospital to make a brief visit to me.

"While Deolinda and I were beginning to think of letting the family know of our approaching return to Balasar, an unexpected obstacle arose. One of the nurses charged with my surveillance had spoken of my case to a physician named Dr Alvaro. Not knowing anything about me, he expressed his immediate disbelief and affirmed that the nurses who were watching me must have been deceived. He added that he would only believe in my fast if it were testified to him by a nurse of his faith.

"Dr Araujo was indignant because it put the seriousness of his study in doubt. He invited Dr Alvaro to send a nurse of his own choice and the latter selected one of his sisters. I was therefore asked to remain in the hospital for an additional period of observation.

"The new test lasted ten days – and with what suspicion! When my sister, with Dr Alvaro's permission, entered my room every evening to turn me, the new nurse lit the light and stood beside her. As soon as Deolinda left, the nurse ... made a rigorous check to ascertain if Deolinda had concealed something under the sheets.

"Nor did they lack subterfuges to induce me to eat something which the assistant nurse always had with her. When she showed me some tasty morsels, I smiled without saying anything and when she offered them to me, I thanked her and still smiling, pretended not to understand her. Frequently, all my linen was taken away to be inspected. The nurse who assisted me during those last ten days became convinced of the reality of my fast and afterwards visited my home where she greeted me like a dear friend.

"On 19 July 1943, the eve of my discharge, all the children of the hospital passed around my bed and I prayed with them. Later more than 1,500 people came and the authorities had to call the police to maintain order. One policeman limited himself to standing by my bed and saying continually to the crowd who pressed around, 'Pass along, pass along.' The doctor had to literally implore the crowd that pressed round the entrance to the hospital and in my room to move back so that I would not be suffocated. I remained humiliated, exhausted and full of self-contempt for the tears of the visitors and for the many kisses I received which I did not merit and did not want.

"On the morning of my departure, Dr Araujo rose early as usual and told me that he had been unable to sleep that night due to the responsibility weighing on him. When he arrived at the hospital, a crowd awaited him. After spending a short while with me, he permitted some people to enter the hospital and only then did he tell us that we were free and that the 'observation' was ended. He allowed my sister to eat a meal near me and then said, 'In October, I will come to visit you at Balasar, not as a doctor-spy, but as a friend who esteems you.'

"I kissed the doctor's hand gratefully and thanked him from my heart. I did this in all sincerity for I was deeply grateful to him for the seriousness with which he had treated my case."

So ends Alexandrina's account of the medical investigation of her fast. The official report issued by Dr Araujo confirmed the prodigy as "scientifically inexplicable". The key sentence stated: "It is absolutely certain that during forty days of being bedridden in hospital, the sick woman did not eat or drink . . . and we believe such phenomenon could have happened during the past months, perhaps the past 13 months . . . leaving us perplexed." The report is signed Dr Gomez de Araujo of the Royal Academy of Medicine, Madrid, specialist in nervous diseases and arthritis.

In addition to the formal medical report, there was a certificate signed by Drs Lima and Azevedo. It read as follows:

> We the undersigned, Dr C. A. di Lima, Professor of the Faculty of Medicine of Oporto and Dr E. A. D. de Azevedo, doctor graduate of the same Faculty, testify that, having examined Alexandrina Maria da Costa, aged 39, born and resident at Balasar, of the district of Povoa de Varzim . . . have confirmed her paralysis. . . . And we also testify that the bedridden woman, from 10 June to 20 July 1943 remained in the sector for infantile paralysis at the Hospital of Foce del Duro, under the direction of Dr Araujo and under the day and night surveillance by impartial persons desirous of discovering the truth of her fast. Her abstinence from solids and liquids was *absolute* during all that time. We testify also that she retained her weight, and her temperature, breathing, blood pressure, pulse and blood were normal while her mental faculties were constant and lucid and she had not, during these forty days, any natural necessities.

The certificate continues:

> The examination of the blood, made three weeks after her arrival in the hospital, is attached to this certificate and from it one sees how, considering the aforesaid abstinence from solids and liquids, science naturally has no explanation. The laws of physiology and biochemistry cannot account for the survival of this sick woman for forty days of absolute fast in the hospital, more so in that she replied daily to many interrogations and sus-

tained very many conversations, showing an excellent disposition and a perfect lucidity of spirit. As for the phenomena observed every Friday at about 3 p.m. (i.e. her ecstasies), we believe they belong to the mystical order. . . . For the sake of the truth, we have prepared this certificate which we sign. Oporto, 26 July 1943.

A distinguished professor who carefully examined the medical reports and other details of the examinations made on Alexandrina testified:

In returning to my friend and client (i.e. Fr Pinho) the copies of the reports concerning the singular case of Alexandrina Maria da Costa, I desire to thank him for the opportunity he has offered me of studying in minute detail this strange case. . . . It was above all as a doctor, specialist in nutrition, and not only as a Catholic, that I found that which had happened to the sick woman so interesting. I also attach great importance to his testimony (i.e. Fr Pinho's report on Alexandrina submitted some years earlier to the Archbishop of Braga), because an enlightened confessor and spiritual director is, perhaps, more competent than anyone else to determine if his subject is mentally normal or abnormal. In my opinion, it is not possible to explain by purely scientific means, or better still, by medical means, that which has happened to Alexandrina da Costa. Nothing makes us believe, according to what one reads in the detailed reports of the doctors and the confessor, that it is simply a matter of hysteria, particularly in view of the long time in which the sick woman has passed, and is still passing, without taking the slightest nourishment. On the other hand, I am certain that it is not a matter of deception because the impartial commission which observed her for forty days and forty nights with rigorous vigilance, could verify that her abstinence from nourishment was total.

He adds,

Now this abstinence from all food during such a long period of time is incompatible with life, and much less with the maintenance of normal temperature, respiration, pulse, blood pressure, etc. . . . Her intellectual life is intense, her relationships are perfect, her faculties and senses are retained in an absolute manner. . . . This extraordinary case, rather I would say exceptional case, can in no way be explained by purely natural means, or through scientific data. The inflammation of the spinal cord, which is most probably the cause of the paralysis, has nothing to do with her abstinence from food, being merely a parallel illness.

This report was signed by Professor Ruj. Joao Marques, professor of medical science, Pernambuco; qualified university lecturer of the faculty of medicine, Recife; professor of the branch of nutrition of the School of Social Service, Pernambuco; president of the Society of Gastroenterology and Nutrition, Pernambuco.

So much for the verdict of medical science. But Alexandrina had a succinct explanation. She confided to her confessor that Our Lord had told her, "You are living by the Eucharist alone because I want to prove to the world the power of the Eucharist and the power of my life in souls."

8

Seraph of love

Alexandrina's joy at returning home was unfortunately short-lived. A letter arrived from Fr Pinho explaining with deep regret that his heavy commitments in other parts of the country made it virtually impossible for him to continue as her spiritual director. The shock was severe, but worse was to follow. Her physical condition sharply deteriorated again, and by the end of 1943 her pain had once more reached an intolerable degree. Groaning in agony and sorely stricken over the loss of her spiritual director, she gasped to Deolinda that this was surely the end. After receiving the last sacraments, she passed through a second mystical death — a protracted spasm of blinding pain which manifested a kind of breakdown and incineration of her body. The sight of such unspeakable suffering brought tears of compassion to the eyes of endless files of pilgrims who came to implore a share in her unceasing prayers. Among them was her former employer who broke down at the sight of her pitiful condition. "She is a saint", he wept. "And to think she is crucified on that bed of pain through my fault."

Her repeated ecstasies seemed to intensify with her appalling suffering. In her autobiography she wrote of experiencing the indescribable torments of hell and purgatory. Her long description of the former echoes the terrifying vision of hell seen by the three Fatima children on 13 July 1917 and recorded by Sister Lucia. Of purgatory, Alexandrina wrote:

> On the Feast of Christ the King 1943, I felt that my body had died and that my existence on earth had ended completely. Words fail to express the sorrow I felt at

that moment. What sufferings, my God, what sufferings were these! I was feeling flames passing through me. I seemed to feel their terrible heat due to the great thirst I was suffering. But I was mistaken. Those flames continue still. They were not flames of this world. They had a brightness that was enchanting. They were passing through me for hours together, torturing my senses. They were rising to great heights ... causing me indescribable pain, but in spite of that, I was compelled to plunge into them in order to purify myself by them.

These agonies were intensified by her continuous interior suffering of the Passion of Our Lord which had begun on Good Friday 1942 and which was to persist until her death. The pain she experienced was even more acute than in the earlier Passion ecstasies, but she never left her bed. Occasionally, her dreadful torments were punctuated by shafts of ecstatic relief. On 5 August 1944 for instance, she wrote of Our Lord entering and taking possession of her tortured body, allowing her soul to escape from its fiery prison of pain to spend a day of ineffable joy in heaven. But the radiance soon faded and she returned to find herself once again locked in a furnace of agony.

Seeing her so desolate, several friends of the family implored a noted Salesian priest, Fr Umberto Pasquale, who was stationed some 90 miles to the south, to visit her and bring her what comfort he could. The Salesian hesitated, mainly because malicious stories were still circulating about Alexandrina's fast, despite the medical confirmation. Finally Fr Pinho, who was at the other side of the country, wrote and persuaded him to go, insisting that her fast and mysticism were absolutely genuine.

Fr Pasquale needed no second prompting; he journeyed to Balasar at once and after spending two days with the seer, realised the extraordinary calibre of her soul. During a second visit, he asked her for a share in her prayers and sufferings. She replied, "How can I *not* do that if you are my second spiritual director?" The priest was taken aback by this unexpected answer and decided first to consult Fr

Pinho. The latter reassured him and urged him to accept. "She is yours", he added. "I entrust her to you. Our Lord will give you the light to guide her."

The Salesian was satisfied and took up his task at once. "I confess that it was a great relief for me", Fr Pinho later admitted, "in seeing how Providence so competently supplied Alexandrina's deficiency in the person of Fr Umberto Pasquale, master of Salesian novices, preacher and writer. In the most difficult circumstances, he was to give the sick woman an assiduous and enlightening direction." [Cf. *On the Calvary of Balasar* by Fr Mariano Pinho, SJ.]

Aware of the delicate task of guiding such an exceptional soul, Fr Pasquale prayed long and earnestly for the prudence and wisdom that had been given to his predecessor. He began by requesting Alexandrina in September 1944 to write down everything that had happened in her life to enable him to gain a deeper understanding of her mysticism. Over the following years, she dictated to Deolinda some 5,000 pages of typescript, which completed her autobiography. This comprises one of the most important documents at present under study in Rome in connection with her cause for beatification.

Fr Pasquale also asked if she would devote part of her sufferings and continuous prayers for the salvation of youth. She responded immediately and on 26 February 1945, she became a Salesian cooperator. In this capacity, she offered up her constant pain and prayers in union with Salesians all over the world for the salvation of souls, particularly those of young people, and for the sanctification of cooperators everywhere. The Salesians were so impressed by her courage and willingness that they gave her a unique diploma of membership. When Fr Pasquale presented it to her, she asked for it to be placed by her bed "so that I can always have sight of it".

Her generous and enthusiastic participation in her work as a Salesian cooperator inspired the fathers so much that they gave her a beautiful white satin lily made in the Carmel of Fatima, to be placed in her hand after death. On receiving

In 1945 Alexandrina became a Salesian Cooperator. Thus she offered up her constant pain and prayers in union with members of the Salesian order all over the world for the salvation of souls, particularly those of young people, and for the sanctification of Cooperators everywhere.

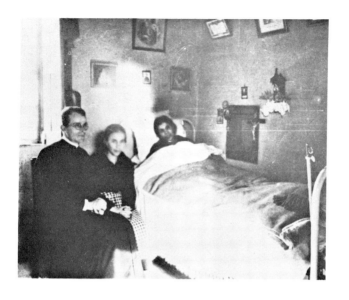

Alexandrina with her sister Deolinda and her second spiritual director, Father Umberto Pasquale. This picture was taken in 1946.

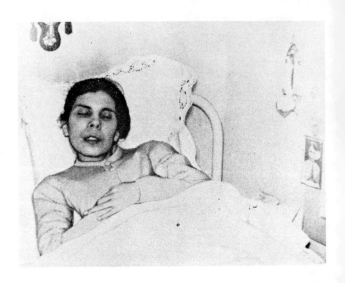

Alexandrina in ecstasy in 1948, at age forty-four. On the wall is
a picture of Jacinta Marto, one of the three seers of Fatima.
Alexandrina often drew her visitors' attention to this picture
and urged them to follow Jacinta's heroic example of sacrifice.

Alexandrina said, "Would that I could set the whole world on fire with the love of Jesus and Mary!"

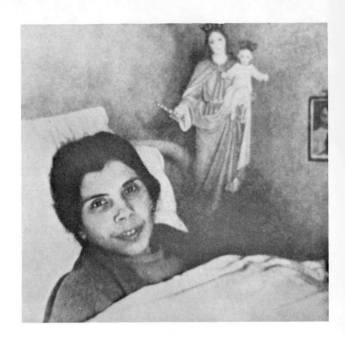

Thousands of pilgrims flocked to Alexandrina, hoping to see her, to speak with her, and to implore her prayers.

it from her director she smiled through her pain and stammered, "I am so happy with this lily. . . . But as I do not merit it, what must I do? If I regard my merit, I would not receive anything." Deolinda turned it round for her so that she could read on the leaves some of her past utterances regarding her longing to make Eucharistic reparation and to immolate herself for sinners. A silk ribbon was tied to the stem of the lily on which was written: "The Salesians to their Cooperator."

To demonstrate her affection for the Salesians in a tangible way, she wrote little spiritual letters to them and their novices in her own hand. Commenting on the significance of this, Fr Pasquale observed, "Only God knows what it must have cost her. We are witness to the fact that the writing of a simple thought on the back of a holy picture wrung the sweat from her brow and made her almost faint with pain."

The following letter was characteristic:

Jesus lives!
My dear novices and Salesians of so holy a house, I would like to write to each one of you, but I cannot. I lack the strength. But as it is my duty to thank you for your holy prayers on my behalf, I thank you all together. Jesus and his Mother will repay you for such charity. I implore from Heaven the blessings and graces of Our Lord. I only desire that you occupy in the Divine Heart of Jesus the same place which you occupy in mine, because in this way you will be able to receive everything. I have you all so much inside my heart. May God reward all those who have written to me. You can be certain that Jesus will give you all you desire for your sanctification and for the salvation of souls.

Trust, trust; Jesus will always be with you! Count always on me on earth and afterwards in Heaven where I will wait for you. In charity, pray for me.

I am,
poor Alexandrina.

Another time she sent a pious picture to the Salesians with these words on the reverse:

For all the Salesians — Balasar 1.4.1945.
Among all, be the smallest. Blind obedience. Never sin.
Suffer in silence. Love Jesus. Love, only love!
                                        poor Alexandrina Maria.

Meanwhile her profound ecstasies continued. As many of these startling raptures are under investigation in Rome in connection with her cause for beatification, final judgment on them must be reserved. Like a few of the greatest mystical saints, she underwent a mystical marriage with Jesus[1] and was crowned a queen by Our Lady.[2] The following year her heart was exchanged with Our Lord's Sacred Heart as happened to St Margaret Mary.[3] She heard him pronounce her "blessed of my Father", and received the ineffable privilege of contemplating the Most Holy Trinity.[4] Soon after, a wondrous ecstasy manifested her transformation into Christ.[5] Aglow with a seraphic love of Jesus and his mother, she underwent sublime raptures of the Resurrection and Ascension into heaven[6] and was pierced by darts of unspeakable love from a flight of angels.

Early in the 1950s, Alexandrina was grievously wounded by a mystical stigmata of love, as happened to St Catherine of Siena. To awed witnesses crowding her little room, she seemed to be literally transfigured in a divine glow. In a blaze of agony and adoring love, she panted forth the rapture of her life mission in ecstatic tones: "Would that I could set the whole world on fire with the love of Jesus and Mary!"

And Our Lord reputedly told her:

If you knew how much I love you, you would die of joy. I have established my home in your soul. I live in you as if you alone exist in the world and I had only you to

---

1. 8 December 1944.   4. 13 August 1945.
2. First Saturday of December 1944.   5. 1 September 1945.
3. 11 May 1945.   6. 4-16 January 1946.

bless. You are a tabernacle constructed by divine hands. I want you in my arms with the same simplicity of a baby in those of its mother. Give me your heart to place in mine in order that you will have no other love but for me and for the things that are mine. In your body is Christ; Christ in your glances and in your smiles. You are the valley and I the water which flows in it, which washes and purifies. You are rich in me. It is because of this that your glances attract. It is because of this that your smile has the fineness of Heaven. I want you to preach devotion to the tabernacles. I want you to kindle in souls devotion to this Prisoner of Love. I do not stay in this world only for love of those who love me, but for everyone. Even those engaged in work can console me.

After each ecstasy, the dreadful pain would close in again; for long periods during the late 1940s she endured appalling tortures to atone for various categories of sins. She could not bear to hear others pronounce the words *sin* and *sinners,* even in the Hail Mary, without shuddering violently.

This phenomenon had been noticed for many years and was highlighted by an incident which took place on 26 December 1938. She was visited by a medical specialist who treated her with much cruelty. "He wanted to force me to sit on a chair", she recalled in her autobiography, "and he tried to move me from the bed with all his strength. . . . I suffered horribly, banging my head on the wall."

Unable to succeed, he then said to Alexandrina: "Say the Hail Mary." When she showed no sign of shuddering at the word *sinners,* he gave her a little slap on the cheek and said, "You see, I have caught you out. You said *sinner –*" He checked abruptly, seeing her tremble convulsively. He then pinned her arms and tried his utmost to stop the movement, but was unable to succeed. Moments later, he was flung into the air. Picking himself up, he went to consult Fr. Pinho in the next room. The priest explained that the strange phenomenon did not happen when *she* pronounced the word "sin" or "sinner" — only when others did.

During this period, she corresponded regularly with Sister Lucia, the last survivor of the three Fatima children, and Fr Pasquale became confidant to some of the mysteries of the world beyond the grave.

To a world splintering to pieces with broken Commandments, Our Lord pleaded to Alexandrina for more victim souls to turn the scales of divine justice. She would pass on his words to the thousands of pilgrims who flocked to see her, adding that she felt she was shouldering a mountainous burden almost alone. She would cry out in anguish that she felt literally poisoned by humanity's sins. Once again she was tormented by the unendurable odour of sin, as happened after her first Passion ecstasy in 1938. And all this time she was continually examined by doctors and theologians who left profoundly stirred. On one occasion, an atheist doctor staggered from her room with the light of faith in his eyes.

One morning while she was asking Our Lady to prepare her soul for Holy Communion, she felt a sudden sense of supernatural peace. She recalled:

> My eyes were open, and I began to see in front of me a crowd of angels forming a great arch. Opposite stood a throne ablaze with radiant colours emitting rays of light. Our Lord explained that he had presented this vision to me to show that my prayers were heard in Heaven. "It was the Virgin and my angels, Cherubim and Seraphim, who came down to prepare your soul. They have thanked and praised me as in Heaven. I am on a throne inside you."

The aura of sanctity surrounding Alexandrina was fast duplicating that of the famous Italian stigmatist Padre Pio, and was intensified by the conviction that she radiated a supernatural fragrance. Once Fr Pasquale brought his sister to visit Alexandrina for a few days. She spent the night in an adjoining room and being very emotional after having witnessed one of the seer's Friday ecstasies, she was unable to sleep. All through the night however, she was conscious of delicious waves of perfume coming from Alexandrina's room next door. The following morning she asked her brother for the name of the perfume used by the seer. Unable to tell her and because he had previously noticed it himself, he asked Deolinda. She smiled and replied, "We don't use perfume. Do you think that this, the poorest house in the country, would be a house for perfume?"

Fr Pasquale understood then. The incredibly beautiful fragrance could not possibly be of this world. It was like a breath of paradise. The strange phenomenon persisted for years. Hundreds of people noticed it, even at a distance of 150 km. in the Salesian House of Fr Pasquale. Often the church and courtyard were filled with the same delectable odour causing much comment among the students. The priests pretended to ignore it, but were finally compelled to draw up a signed deposition testifying to the reality of the fragrance.

Unaware of all this, Alexandrina then had an ecstasy in which Our Lord reportedly told her:

> Tell your director that he was chosen by me to come here to study, support and defend my divine work. Tell him that the perfume is a divine aroma; it is the perfume of your virtue. I am disclosing this because he has need of it for the report which he is making of your case.

A priest who visited Alexandrina at this time came away with an extraordinary story. As he blessed her, he suddenly saw before him the sorrowful face of Jesus in place of the sick woman. He testified afterwards, "It was not an illusory impression — it was a vision which lasted some minutes." He felt that he had been struck by lightning and went away weeping bitterly for his sins.

Stories like these predictably increased the already large crowds flooding into Balasar and besieging Alexandrina's humble home. Despite her deep-rooted desire for a life of seclusion and private prayer, she accepted the clear call of God and devoted all her scant energy to succouring the spiritual needs of the pilgrims. "Sinners and Alexandrina were inseparable ends of a heavenly mission", Fr Pasquale observed. "She exerted a sweet and mysterious force that subdued them all." Unable to think or speak of sin without feeling a sense of disintegration, she strove to reform the innumerable sinners who crowded her little room. She felt an inexpressible compassion for them. "When they tell me of their wretchedness," she wrote, "I feel I want to embrace them." She recalled that Jesus himself was the inseparable friend of sinners.

Her gaze was so full of pity that many would break down and weep at her mere glance. Those intending to visit her would first go to confession, knowing that they would otherwise be unable to bear her penetrating look. It was not a gaze to frighten the guilty, but to move them to tears of grief for their sins and to awaken in them a powerful resolve to amend their lives, to confess and return to God. "This must surely be the look of Jesus", was the verdict of many.

The prize coveted by most pilgrims was a private talk with the seer. She did her utmost to satisfy as many as she could, listening patiently, counselling, speaking soberly to one individual after another, hour upon hour without a break, always calm and serene and with a glowing smile overlaying the cruel pain striking beneath. By June 1953 she was receiving as many as 6,000 people in a single day, and speaking for ten hours at a time on the message of Fatima. "Make reparation to Our Lord in the Adorable Eucharist! Penitence! Penitence! Penitence! Pray the Rosary devoutly every day. Practice the First Saturday devotion.* Consecrate yourselves to the Immaculate Heart of Mary through the Brown Scapular of Our Lady of Mount Carmel." Asked if she felt tired at the end of the day she murmured, "I could receive as many again." She confessed that she had the feeling of being like a fisherman with many nets to throw to souls.

---

*This devotion was requested by Our Lady at Fatima in 1925 and consists of confession, Communion, rosary and 15 minutes rosary meditation for 5 consecutive Saturdays, with the intention of making reparation to the Immaculate Heart of Mary.

"Sin no more! Sin no more!" The anguish of that stricken cry, echoing in that small dim-lit room, moved even hardened men to tears. Through her, Our Lord promised that "many souls" would become ardently Eucharistic. He added:

You live in my public life. Never have I been far from you since the day of your Baptism. Thousands have been saved by your terrible sufferings. If anyone should invoke your name when you are in Heaven, they will never do so in vain. I appoint you a protectress of mankind. You will be powerful with the All-Powerful. After your death, I will make your name widely known; I shall see to it myself. Many sinners will come to your tomb and be converted. Find souls who will love me in my Sacrament of Love to take your place when you go to Heaven. Invite the world to prayer and penitence that it will be set afire with love for me.

During this arduous, rapturous period, her ecstasies gravitated more towards the state of the Church and the world. She received a piercing gift of prophecy and foretold many events which subsequently happened. "Vanity and extravagance in the world must cease", Our Lord told her. "Let those exhibiting their bodies clothe themselves. Let modesty reign. Penance! Prayer! Much prayer is needed!" Frequently while in ecstasy, Alexandrina was heard lamenting and praying aloud for the Church which she saw in danger of a "great crisis" and threatened by a "wild beast". She was heard quoting our Lord as follows: "Tell my ministers to be vigilant, for the devil is preparing a massive assault on the Church. But pray and trust; victory will be mine."

In the late 1940s, Alexandrina lost her spiritual director, Fr Pasquale, who had been called away on other work. But whenever there was no priest to bring her Communion, our Lord himself reputedly brought her the Sacred Host. On Christmas Day 1953, she had her last public ecstasy – an ineffable vision of the Most Holy Trinity. Sixteen months later, on 9 April 1955, she completed the thirteenth year of her perfect fast. The living miracle of Alexandrina stood as a challenge to this sceptical, self-sufficient age of nuclear energy and computers.

9

Who will sing with the angels?

During the early part of 1955 Alexandrina's condition became critical again. Her dreadful suffering reached a new peak of fearful intensity. Whereas before, during her mystical deaths, it seemed that "birds and beasts" were devouring her body, they now seemed to be devouring her very soul. Month after fiery month she lay quivering and gasping, willingly offering up her frightful torment to atone for mortal sins against faith and hope.

Finally the worst was over and as the ferocious pain eased somewhat, she sighed with deathly exhaustion. On 2 October 1955 she whispered to Deolinda, "Today is the feast of the Angels. This morning I felt someone touch me on the shoulder and I heard a voice saying, 'Who will sing with the angels? You, you, you! In a little while, in a little while.' "

Sensing her imminent departure for heaven, Alexandrina began to prepare her family and friends for the sorrowful separation. Early in the morning of 12 October she asked for her confessor, Don Alberto Gomes, to thank him for all he had done for her, and to ask permission to renew the act of renunciation she had made on Christmas Day 1946. In the evening, Mgr Mendes do Carmo of the diocese of Guarda celebrated Mass in the little room and she received Holy Communion. "As soon as I gave her the Sacred Host", he recalled, "she composed herself in the eloquent and profound silence of her thanksgiving." Deep in her Eucharistic embrace, Alexandrina reputedly heard Our Lord calling her: "My child, receive Extreme Unction if you wish, but come to Heaven, come to Heaven!"

After her thanksgiving, she murmured to Fr Pasquale, who had returned to Balasar to be with her at the end:

> How I long for Heaven! I feel no pain at leaving the world. . . . But while my mind is still clear, I would like to receive Extreme Unction. . . . O how it will all be beautiful here! O Jesus, thy Will be done and not mine.

The parish priest, her confessor, Mgr Mendes, Dr Azevedo, the family and their friends all arrived and went down on their knees. Alexandrina then made her act of renunciation:

> O Jesus, my love! O Divine Spouse of my soul, I, who in life tried only to give you the greatest glory, I wish in the hour of my death to make an act of renunciation to everything and everybody. If with this act I give the greatest praise to the Most Holy Trinity, I submit myself to your eternal designs . . . only imploring from your divine mercy your reign of love, the conversion of sinners, the salvation of the dying and the relief of the souls in Purgatory.

To this she added the act of acceptance of her death. "My God, I have always consecrated my life to you and I offer you now its end, accepting death with resignation, with all its pains, for your greater glory."

In a touching scene, Alexandrina then thanked everyone present for all they had done for her, begging pardon of each one in turn for the trouble she had caused them over so many years. She promised to remember them all in heaven. The parish priest then administered extreme unction. Three times during the moving ceremony, Alexandrina smiled through her interminable pain and her drawn features glowed with an inexpressible joy.

When it was over, she turned to her sobbing relatives and friends and murmured, "Do not weep for mè. I am so happy because I am going to Heaven at last." There was a quivering pause and then all the yearning intensity of her martyred soul broke forth:

> Oh Jesus! I can no longer stay on earth! Oh Jesus, life is dear, Heaven is dear! I have suffered so much in this life

for souls! I am crushed, I am consumed in this bed of pain. Forgive everyone! Pardon, pardon the entire world. . . . Oh I feel so happy! I am so happy because I am going to Heaven at last!

And she raised her feeble eyes with an almost beatific gaze.

As the evening closed in she murmured to Dr Azevedo, "How right you were! What light there is! What light! The darkness is no longer here! It has gone! All is light!"

Early on the morning of the 13th, the 38th anniversary of the final appearance of Our Lady at Fatima and the miracle of the sun, she cried out with passionate fervour, "Oh my God, I love you! I am yours completely! Oh how I long to fly to you! Will it be today? Oh I would be so happy . . . so happy!" A streaming vision of the Immaculate Heart of Mary gently assured her, "I am about to take you." Through the white radiance she heard the voice of Jesus, "You are in the number of my saints", and that of the eternal Father, "This is our well beloved daughter."

As dawn broke, she wore a seraphic smile and asked Deolinda for the crucifix and medal of Our Lady of Sorrows to kiss. When these were brought to her, Deolinda asked, "What are you smiling at now?" And Alexandrina could only murmur, "At Heaven . . . Heaven."

Shortly before 8 a.m. she received Holy Communion again with an overflowing love and devotion. It was her last. Then, as the hushed stillness of the room quivered with praying priests, pilgrims and relatives, she uttered a last piercing message to them and to all mankind in this perilous nuclear age: "Do not sin. The pleasures of this life are worth nothing. Receive Communion, pray the Rosary every day. This sums up everything."

At midday, her trembling joy at the swift approach of paradise burst forth anew. "Oh I am so happy, so happy because I am going to Heaven at last!" The doctor begged her to remember them there and Alexandrina smilingly nodded. She then asked all present to recite the prayers for the dying. These were led by Mgr Mendes on his knees and his moving words seemed to impel that blessed soul forward to the divine embrace.

Her unrelenting agony racked her to the very end, but she withstood the fearful pain with dogged, prayerful fortitude. And as the sun sank in the reddened sky, Alexandrina's life slowly ebbed away. Feebly she kissed the crucifix and medal of Our Lady of Sorrows again. "Goodbye," she whispered almost inaudibly to her weeping relatives, "we will meet again in Heaven." When Deolinda, choking back her sobs, murmured, "Yes, in Heaven . . . but not yet", as if to hold her back a little longer, Alexandrina sighed, by now secure and decisive. "Yes, in Heaven! I am going to Heaven . . . quickly . . . now!"

At 8 p.m. her lips closed to kiss the crucifix for the last time and did not open again. At 8.29 p.m. that heart which had beaten only for love finally ceased.

Around that bed which seemed like an altar, her weeping relatives and friends remained on their knees in prayer. And there came to their minds those moving words which Alexandrina had spoken long ago in 1942 when she seemed to be on the point of death. "When you hear the bells ring for my death, go down on your knees and pray and thank Jesus and Our Lady for coming to take me."

After a long silence, Mgr Mendes, who had not left Alexandrina for two days, drew near to the body and bent reverently to kiss the hands and one by one, the crowded room gradually emptied. The virginal body, white as a flower, was dressed in the garment of a Daughter of Mary. And in the morning when the death bells sounded, the entire countryside was invaded by a sense of mournful sadness. "The mother of the poor is dead," the peasants lamented. "The help of the sorrowful, the consoler of the afflicted has gone."

The news spread rapidly and many thousands from all over Portugal flocked to venerate the body and touch it with pious objects. The people of Balasar dressed themselves in mourning until the Mass of the seventh day, and in the fields where they worked all the singing of the adults and the children was suspended. Alexandrina's death united everyone, rich and poor, great and small, in a visible bond of tears and prayers.

Just before the funeral, the family made public Alexandrina's last directions which she had dictated in 1942.

It is my desire that my funeral may be a poor one, that my coffin may not be very beautiful nor poor in quality, so as not to attract attention from anyone. I wish to be dressed in the gown of a Daughter of Mary, but very modestly. If it is not prohibited by Holy Church, I would like to have on my coffin many flowers, not because I merit them, but because I love them very much. If one takes account of my merit, I would not and could not have anything.

It is my desire to be buried in the earth and without a zinc coffin. I do not want even the official funeral because my mother cannot afford it. On the route of the funeral, I would like the deepest meditation; it has always grieved me to see and hear how funeral retinues display themselves. I do not consent to an autopsy. What they have done to me in life will be quite enough for their studies.

I desire to be buried, if it is possible, with my face turned towards the tabernacle of our church. As in life I always desired to unite myself with Jesus in the Blessed Sacrament and to look at my tabernacle as often as possible, so after my death, I wish to continue my watch, keeping myself turned towards our Eucharistic Lord. I know that with the eyes of my body I will not see Jesus again, but I want to be placed in this position to demonstrate to him the love I have for the Adorable Eucharist.

I would like my tomb to be surrounded by passion flowers to indicate that as I loved sorrow in life, I will continue to love it after my death. Intertwined with the passion flowers, I would like some climbing roses with many thorns. I love and will love the martyrdom that Jesus gave me and the thorns which wounded me. It is with martyrdom and with thorns that we resemble Jesus, that we console his Sacred Heart, and that we save souls, the children of his Precious Blood. What greater proof of love can we give him if not to suffer with joy all that is pain, scorn and humiliation? What greater glory can we give to his Divine Heart than to give him souls for whom he has suffered and given his life?

I would like a cross on my tomb and nearby, an image of Our Lady. If it is possible, I would like a crown of thorns to be placed on the cross. The cross will be a symbol of the suffering I bore and loved until death. Our Lady will be there to say to all that it was she who helped me to complete the sorrowful walk of my Calvary, accompanying and sustaining me until the last moment of my existence. I trust that it will be so. I love Jesus. I love Our Lady. I love suffering. But only in Heaven will I understand the full value of my suffering.

At 10.00 a.m. on 15 October the funeral began. People of all social classes were represented — professors, doctors, lawyers, merchants, industrialists, artists and ordinary working men and women. A newspaper in Oporto reported that "for twenty-one consecutive hours, a vast multitude crowded round the door of the humble home of the Costa family to see for the last time 'the sick woman of Calvary' as she was known to everybody". Some florists in the city were unable to obtain white roses anywhere as every one available had been sent to Balasar.

An eyewitness, D. Ismael de Matos, has left us a graphic account of Alexandrina's extraordinary funeral. "At the head of the funeral cortège stood out the standard of the Apostleship of Prayer on which were painted these words of Jesus, (spoken to St Margaret Mary, 1673), 'Here is the Heart which has so loved men!' " We do not know if the writer was conscious of what Jesus said to Alexandrina on 1 October 1954:

I want you to set fire to the world with this love of my Divine Heart, today extinguished in men's hearts. Set fire! Set fire! I want to give my love to all men. I want to be loved by all. They do not accept it and do not love me.

By you, I want this love to be kindled in all humanity, just as by you the world was consecrated to the Immaculate Heart of my Blessed Mother.

"When according to custom the coffin was opened in the parish church, the people crowded round the bier while tens of priests sang the Office and celebrated Mass. All wanted to touch that body; all wanted to kiss the hands, those hands which, although immobilised for many years through illness, had been a magnetised column raised to Heaven with the power of prayer and suffering, to draw down on earth a stream of mercy and grace.

"During the sacred ceremony in the spacious parish church, it was necessary to create a passage through the dense crowd so that all would be able to look once again on the serenity and sweetness of Alexandrina, on the one who was always resigned and charitable, who received and listened to so many people and petitions.

"Towards one o'clock she was taken to the cemetery in her coffin, which was overwhelmed with flowers. She was buried in a poor and humble tomb, just as her life had been poor and humble, with her face turned towards the tabernacle as she had always desired. The mourning family received visitors, telegrams and letters of condolence from all over the country. It was a unanimous chorus of voices exalting the memory and virtue of Alexandrina."

Two years after her death, the diocesan authorities erected a chapel over her tomb, and in 1967 the Archbishop of Braga, Francisco Maria da Silva, solemnly opened the diocesan investigation into her cause for beatification. On 10 April 1973 it was successfully completed and forwarded to Rome. On that occasion the Archbishop gave a long discourse on the Servant of God, at the end of which he thanked everyone who had taken such pains in the long and meticulous work of the tribunal of the process. His Grace concluded:

The instruments of this work are, above all, the Salesian Fathers. I therefore congratulate you, because

Left: Alexandrina in death. She died at the age of fifty-one, on October 13, 1955, the anniversary of the miracle of the sun at Fatima. Before her death Alexandrina had asked to be buried in the gown of a Daughter of Mary. A vast multitude of thousands from all over Portugal came to the da Costa home to see for the last time "the sick woman of Calvary."

Above: Father Umberto Pasquale, standing by the first tomb of Alexandrina, before translation of her remains to the parish church in 1977. This picture was taken in 1969.

Alexandrina's tomb as it appears today inside St. Eulalia's Church. Engraved on the wall above are some of her most beautiful utterances to the Blessed Sacrament. As she had foretold, her body did not remain incorrupt, but rather it turned to ashes without decomposing — an extraordinary prodigy. The ashes have exuded a celestial fragrance on the several occasions when the vault has been opened.

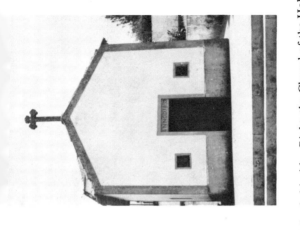

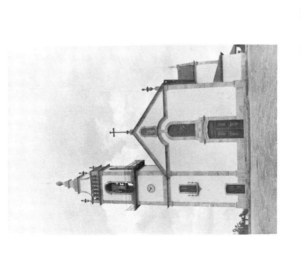

Left: St. Eulalia's parish church in Balasar. Alexandrina is buried inside. *Right:* the Chapel of the Holy Cross, Balasar. This chapel commemorates the mysterious appearance of a cross in the soil in 1832.

The parish church of Balasar with the Chapel of the Holy Cross on the right.

The interior of the parish church of Balasar. On the left is
Alexandrina's tomb.

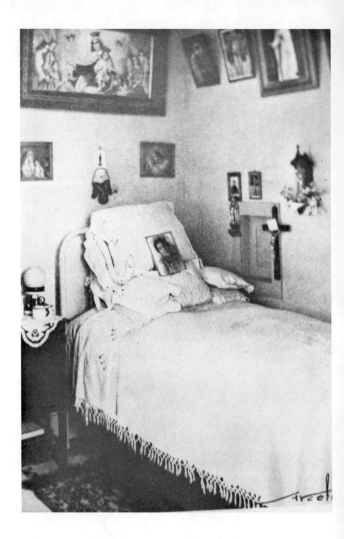

Alexandrina's room as it appears today.

Alexandrina's sister Deolinda and Father Umberto Pasquale,
Alexandrina's second spiritual director. This picture was taken
in August of 1978.

Alexandrina's sister Deolinda with the author, Francis Johnston, on the left, and Father Umberto Pasquale, Alexandrina's
second spiritual director, on the right. In the background are
two Rosary crusaders from England.

Alexandrina was a Salesian Cooperator. I thank you because she was of this diocese – the glory of this diocese. Now I only pray that the Lord may give the opportunity to all of us, or at least to some of us, to assist in the solemn ceremony in the Basilica of St Peter, of the Beatification of Alexandrina; if he should not also wish to give either to all of us, or to some, or to at least one, the glory of assisting in the same Basilica of St Peter, at the Canonisation ceremony of Alexandrina Maria da Costa.

Meanwhile, thousands of pilgrims from all over the world were flocking to her tomb and the little room which was her entire world for over thirty years, "that altar of great sacrifice", as Cardinal Cerejeira epitomised it. Deolinda had not a moment's rest. "It seems that not a day dawns", she wrote, "without seeing people who come to pray at the tomb of my sister. Above all on Sundays and on the 13th of the month there are various pilgrimages from many places." Numerous miracles were reported, both at Balasar and beyond. In 1972, a woman in Southend, England, was reportedly cured of cancer through Alexandrina's intercession. Cardinal Cerejeira himself composed the prayer for her beatification. "The finger of God is here", his Eminence averred, having received "two incredible graces" after praying in the seer's room.

In 1977 the diocesan authorities translated Alexandrina's body from the little chapel to a place of honour beside the high altar of the village church, the Archbishop of Braga deeming it more fitting for her to rest beside her beloved Eucharist. Engraved on the wall above are some of her most beautiful utterances to the Blessed Sacrament. As she had foretold earlier her body was not preserved but had turned to ashes without decomposing – an extraordinary prodigy which has apparently hastened her cause for beatification. The ashes themselves have exuded a celestial fragrance on the several occasions when the vault has been opened.

The church and its immediate vicinity are undergoing extensive structural modifications to accommodate the growing crowds. In August 1978, it was my great privilege to meet Deolinda at Alexandrina's house. Now eighty and in the early stages of Parkinson's disease, she manifested a wonderful kindness and gentleness that gave me an inkling of the sublime devotion she had borne for her saintly sister. And by an exceptional coincidence, Fr Pasquale had just arrived from Turin for a few days after visiting his close friend Sister Lucia, now a Carmelite nun at Coimbra, en route. His cordiality knew no bounds. After showing me everything of interest in the house and explaining how Alexandrina's life is being translated into many languages, he gave me as a precious relic the handkerchief she used just before she died. In answer to my suggestion that Alexandrina may one day prove to be a second St Margaret Mary Alacoque, he gave a most emphatic yes.

Years earlier, in 1948, Alexandrina had dictated her epitaph, a last imploring heart-cry to this permissive age. The words have been engraved on a white marble slab covering her tomb, and they echo the final plea of Our Lady of Fatima on 13 October 1917: "Do not offend God any more, for he is already too greatly offended."

Sinners: if the ashes of my body can be useful to save you, approach. If necessary, pass on the ashes, trample on them until they disappear; but never sin again. Sinners: there is so much that I would like to tell you. This vast cemetery could not contain all that I would like to say. Do not offend our dear Lord any more. Convert yourselves. Do not lose Jesus for all eternity. He is so good.
Enough of sin!
LOVE HIM! LOVE HIM!